Masterguide to Leasing for Retail Landlords

Advanced Techniques to Increase Income & Value While Reducing Risk

Peter D. Morris CRX, SCLS, SCSM, SCMD

First Edition

Greenstead Media,Mill Bay, BC, Canada

i

Printed in Canada.

277 pages

First edition: 2014

Masterguide to Leasing for Retail Landlords – First Edition

ISBN 978-0-9938774-1-4

Greenstead Media
2562 Kinnoull Cresc,
Mill Bay, BC V0R 2P1

Cover image provided courtesy of Grosvenor Americas

Contents

Part 1 The DNA of the Deal

Part 2 Negotiating Key Terms

Part 3 Negotiating the Lease Wording

Part 4 Special Considerations

Important Notice to Readers

Laws are constantly changing. Every effort is made to keep this publication as current as possible. However, the author, the publisher, and the vendor of this book make no representations or warranties regarding the outcome or the use to which the information in this book is put and or not assuming any liability for any claims, losses, or damages arising out of the use of this book. The reader should not rely on the author or the publisher of this book for any professional advice. Please be sure that you have the most current edition.

This book deals with the business concepts, consequences and aspects of commercial real estate leases and commercial real estate leasing. Different laws in different locales will affect commercial leases and leasing differently. Not all concepts outlined in this book may apply in your specific jurisdiction, given your governing laws. Although commercial leases are by their very nature legal documents, and the business practices surrounding the leases touch on aspects of law and legal regulations, the author and publisher are not providing any legal advice. The reader is strongly encouraged to discuss the concepts in this book with a competent legal advisor who is a specialist in commercial real estate leases.

As all leases have a financial impact on the investment in the commercial real estate, it is also important to consult with an accountant who is familiar with the specific accounting practices concerning commercial real estate. The author and publisher are not providing any financial or investment advice.

Foreword by John Andrew, Ph.D.

Director, Queen's Real Estate Roundtable &
Continuing Adjunct Assistant Professor,
School of Urban and Regional Planning &
School of Business
Queen's University, Kingston, Ontario,
Canada

A central tenet in commercial real estate which I am constantly driving home to my students (who are invariably more familiar with residential real estate) is that the value of a building is determined nearly entirely by its ability to generate income. The function of leasing, and the lease itself, are the vehicles by which revenue is realized. Paradoxically, these are ignored in a great many commercial real estate books; even some otherwise excellent ones. So much so that until reading this manuscript, I was not fully aware of what a chasm in the literature it fills.

This book places a strong emphasis on negotiation strategies for designing very specific components of a lease agreement. It makes a cogent argument that the lease provides a great opportunity to increase the value of a property. The multiplier effect of the capitalization (or "cap") rate means that a small change in the value of a lease can have a great effect on the value of a building.

There is also an emphasis on retail leases, but given their added complexity this is appropriate and not overdone.

Peter Morris draws on his vast professional experience in leasing and approaches the lease from the perspective of the building owner. He demonstrates throughout the book specific ways in which a well-designed and clearly written lease maximizes property value and minimizes the risk of conflict, which may escalate into costly litigation. His generous use of examples from real situations he has been involved in keeps the book interesting and helps the reader draw connections between theory and practice. Many of these include hypothetical dialogue between players that is both realistic and effective as a teaching tool. This technique is also illustrative of the plain and clear language that Morris uses throughout.

A convincing observation of the book is that a lease defines how risk is shared between the landlord and tenants. Mr. Morris' characterization of risk factors using a customized "SWOT" (strengths, weaknesses, opportunities and threats) is as helpful as it is creative.

Peter Morris draws connections between leases and other facets of commercial real estate operations that are not normally perceived as related. One example is how he illustrates ways in which a well-written lease may be used as an effective marketing tool to attract and retain tenants. This is part of what he refers to a "Story to Sell"™, and it serves as one of the valuable ways in which the book reframes both commercial properties and their leases in unique and interesting ways.

Peter Morris provocatively asserts that there is only one honest answer to most questions in commercial real estate: "It depends." He builds on this by systematically going through a tremendous number of variables on which many key questions real estate professionals regularly encounter (and a few rare ones). His book takes a very pragmatic approach, replete with hands-on advice such as the section entitled "Top 10 Lease Negotiating Errors." Mr. Morris' information is as current as it is comprehensive, as evidenced by his discussion of the various components of a lease and current trends in leasing.

Readers will benefit greatly from several sections of this book that are unique in the literature: how to make the most prudent and cost-effective use of professionals such as lawyers, accountants and brokers; methods of determining appropriate rent levels (including retail percentage rent from a landlord's strategic negotiating viewpoint); the importance of renewing a *tenancy*, not a *lease*; structuring "use" clauses; crafting effective "green" leases; and how to write good leases for mixed-use developments.

I am certain this book will make a valuable contribution to the professional literature on commercial real estate. There is a tremendous need for high-quality and practical guidance, informed by a level of experience Mr. Morris brings. I know you enjoy it and find it useful.

Introduction

This book is for investors, asset managers, property managers, leasing agents and those aiming to increase the income and value of their retail property.

Why was it written? Unfortunately, there are very few opportunities to learn how to craft superior leasing strategies and the leases themselves. Learning these skills is usually by trial and error. This can be expensive and stressful as mistakes can have repercussions for years after the negotiation. For example, in one chapter I discuss three real life errors that caused an investor to forfeit millions of dollars through the foreclosure of his property.

The reader will gain leading edge knowledge and a standard to which to strive when negotiating and drafting documents.

The book is divided into four main areas:
1. **Advanced leasing**

2. **Negotiating key business terms**

3. **Understanding and negotiating lease wording of key clauses and documenting ancillary events.**

4. **Special leasing considerations for Green leases and Mixed-Use projects**

Each chapter provides specific strategies to create higher returns from the retail property. The Masterguide is illustrated by actual examples of successes and failures in lease negotiations and the importance of the wording of the lease.

I have listed some important guidelines before proceeding.

- Please read the page marked 'Important Notice Readers'.

- If you find any specific idea or concept in this book that does not directly apply to you, it may still be applied to and adapted to your circumstances.

- Leasing practices vary from city to city, and country to country. The concepts in this book are primarily designed for anywhere that has a lease concept versus an owner/occupier concept. That said, modifications may need to be made to fit local laws, customs and standards. For example, the idea of the landlord obtaining more rent from a tenant for each dollar of sales above a certain sales volume (known as percentage or sales or overage rent) does not work in practice in some parts of the world. Cultural differences need to be understood and taken into consideration.

- Throughout the book we refer to the 'landlord'. However, anyone involved in ownership, leasing and management of the property is also included when we say landlord. In many cases, those charged with leasing and management are neither the landlord nor owner or investor.

- If you are a leasing agent, asset manager, property manager, accountant or lawyer you can demonstrate the value of your services to the landlord by using some or all of the experienced, well tried concepts and approaches in this book. You will then be in a position of advantage to both your employer and client. You will have the improved negotiating strength that results in more income to the owner, better long term investment value and decreased risk.

- If you are the investor or landlord, the material in this book will give you the opportunity to structure better lease negotiations. Well negotiated and drafted leases provide more rent, higher returns and greater value at less cost and risk.

Acknowledgements

This book and the expertise I've gained could not have been possible without the help and assistance of dozens of people from around the world who are as passionate about commercial real estate as I am. It would be impossible to properly acknowledge them all. However, a few people stand out as mentors as well as those who have challenged my comprehension and understanding of the business through their unselfish sharing of their knowledge, successes and failures, insightful questions, negotiating styles and patience.

Michael A. Morris CSM. A shopping centre developer, manager, leasing agent and consultant who started in the shopping centre business in the early 1960s; and, more importantly, my father who never shied away from exposing me to the business from an early age and then went on to encourage my growth in the industry.

Alan Stangroom CSM, who hired me for my first management position and took the time to explain every aspect of the business in great detail and allowed me to try new things.

Celia Green, one of the most intelligent people I've ever met and a client for 12 years who challenged my basic lease concepts that allowed for a fresh view of what real estate is truly all about.

Gordon Sustrik, Deborah Lloyd, Steven Messinger, Dennis Daoust, Natalie Vukovich, Howard Kline and other fine attorneys specializing in commercial real estate from whom I discovered the nuances of lease wording.

Mark Taylor, Don Rogers and Brian Castle who are some of the toughest, smartest and most persuasive negotiators on the planet.

George Chambers CCIM, CPM, RPA of the Woodland Chambers Group and Deborah Moore of Riser Realty, friends who told me this book must be written.

Rosemary Morris, who read and edited the manuscript and improved the end product.

Finally, but by no means least, my family - Jane, Amanda and Michael – who completely support my lifelong passion for the industry, my desire to share often hard fought insights and listened to my tales of lament with as much interest as the tales of success.

Chapter 1
THE IMPORTANCE OF
A GREAT LEASE
'The lease, and only the lease,
drives value'

Here is the most unrecognized fact that
impacts everything about leasing. Investors
in a retail property don't actually buy the
real estate. That is not their primary focus.
Instead they are buying the existing and
potential cash flow and profit from the
leases. And the leases are secured by the
covenants of the tenants. The better the
lease and the more stable the tenant to be
able to fulfill the lease terms, the better the
value.

In the acquisition due diligence process
considerable time, energy and effort are
spent verifying the quality of the leases and
the income. The potential purchaser looks at
the quality of the income, the covenants of
the tenants and the quality of the lease
documents. They use any diminishment

from the ideal to discount the income and the purchase price. At the same time, the potential purchaser is looking at opportunities to capitalize on improvements to the leasing they can make.

They also look at the risks associated with the real estate itself. They ask themselves questions such as the need for capital expenses, deferred maintenance, ongoing cost of operation, etc.

As you can see, the leases represent the investment opportunity but the real estate represents the risks to that opportunity.

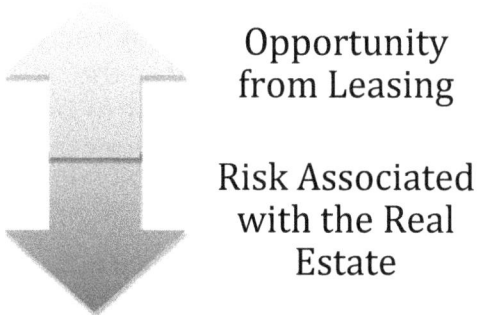

Opportunity
from Leasing

Risk Associated
with the Real
Estate

Anyone who mostly focuses on the real estate itself misses a significant opportunity to increase returns and value by improving the quality of the leasing negotiating process and documentation. That bears repeating:

Anyone (other than the facilities management professionals, whose job is to efficiently manage the physical real estate asset) who spends the majority of their time, attention and efforts on the physical real estate – the building and the lands - and not on improving the quality of the lease transaction and lease management is not adding value or improving returns.

Improving the leasing process adds more incremental value to the owner than cost savings, because there is always more potential upside to improving income than can be found in cost savings.

To illustrate the point, consider that only so much can be saved through cost reduction. Eventually, in an ideal situation, the property would have no costs associated with it. Reality suggests that will never be the case.

Conversely, improving income has no limit.

How $1.00 Equals $20.00

It is vitally important in the highly leveraged business of commercial real estate to understand the impact of a dollar gained or lost in a lease transaction. Commercial real estate is sold and purchased based on the percentage yield the net operating income provides in comparison to the purchase price. As a result, $1.00 can have a significant affect on the value of the asset, all other items remaining equal.

To understand how this occurs, we use the IRV formula. This method converts the income of a property into an estimate of its value. The basic formula is:

Net operating income (I) ÷ capitalization rate (R) = value (V)

Where:

The **net operating income** (NOI) is all revenues less operating expenses exclusive of debt servicing, income taxes, and other non-operating expenses.

The **capitalization rate** (also called the CAP Rate) is the yield of the income based upon a 100% cash purchase price. Stated differently, it is the annual return produced by the net operating income (NOI). Therefore it is expressed as a percentage.

And the **value** is the purchase price.

Because the NOI is divided by the CAP Rate, there is an inverse and compounding effect on value, as shown in the table below, that shows the value of $1 at various CAP Rates.

THE VALUE OF $1 AT VARIOUS CAP RATES*

CAP RATE	VALUE IMPACT
4%	$25.00
5%	$20.00
6%	$16.67
7%	$14.29

*Cap Rates can also be in decimal increments. IE: 6.35%

Therefore, every dollar gained or lost has a significant affect on value.

Here is a practical example in action. Let's assume that the property was recently appraised using a CAP Rate of 6%, and the landlord increased the net operating income from a 1,500 sf premise through good negotiation by $2.50 per square foot per annum (psfpa).

($2.50 X 1,500) ÷ 6% = $62,500.00

The annual NOI increased by $3,750, but the value of the asset has increased by $62,500 on just that one transaction. Conversely, missing the opportunity to increase the NOI by $2.50 psfpa cost the landlord $62,500 in value that could be added to a sale price, added to a refinancing package, etc.

There are only two variables in the IRV formula. The NOI and the CAP Rate.

The CAP rate is determined by a number of factors, most of which the landlord has little control over; such as market conditions, returns from other investment vehicles, etc. It is true however, that a property with an assurance of the NOI will have a lower CAP rate than a property that is more speculative. While the landlord can't control the general market or the economy, they can control their own business actions, quality of the leases they create, etc.

On the other hand, the landlord has far more control over their NOI. Most of that control is achieved through the quality of the leasing, the negotiating and the lease document.

What Makes a Good Lease?

There are two aspects to a good lease. The first is the structure of the lease transaction, or the DNA of the Deal. The second is the quality of the documentation of that transaction.

Many people believe that a good negotiation produces a win/win outcome. While desirable, this is rarely the case. It is because the lease negotiation is more than just the basic financial terms such as rent, length of lease, etc. The balance of the transaction is all about the transfer of risk from one party to the other.

The landlord wants to transfer as much business risk to the tenant as possible, while the tenant wants to transfer its risk to the landlord. Whichever party in the transaction has the negotiating power will transfer the most risk. Some of the most negotiated clauses in a lease have their roots in this concept of risk transfer. For example, the landlord will want to negotiate a reasonable lease term that allows it to finance the property effectively while reserving the opportunity to improve its future financial position. On the other hand, the tenant wants to give itself the most flexibility in reserving its location AND ending the lease if it deems that is in its best interest. The end result may be that the landlord obtains term, but the tenant has certain termination rights to end the lease early.

A successful lease transaction is one where both parties believe they can accept the level of business risk they have each agreed to in the negotiation. The negotiation will conclude only when both the landlord and tenant have reached that point.

In the next chapter we will discuss the art and science of lease negotiations in greater detail. You will learn how to retain as much negotiating strength as possible and to minimize the risk transference from the tenant to the landlord. After all, it is the landlord who has the greatest investment in the real estate and each transaction.

Another, but less recognized, aspect of the concept of risk transfer is in the quality of the documentation.

A well-negotiated and documented lease is a thing of beauty. It almost goes without saying that the final lease should be concise and written in clear language that leaves little room for misunderstanding. Unfortunately, that isn't always the case, as you will see in the chapter about 'trap door' clauses.

An old joke aptly notes the flaw in a poorly worded lease clause and the implications it can have. It is from a vintage Saturday Night Live skit performed in 1984 and it demonstrates how ambiguous language can be. It goes something like this:

They were the parting words of a nuclear engineer turning over a new, sophisticated power plant to the two people who would operate the plant after he left. He said; "The most important thing to remember is that you can never put too much water into this nuclear cooling chamber."

Within an hour of his departure an alarm in the cooling chamber sounded. One operator said to the other; "Remember you can never put too much water into this cooling chamber, so lets add water."

"No", said the other operator, "He said you can never put too much water into this cooling chamber. There must be too much in the system, so lets take some water out."

Thus ensued a heated argument about what to do next until the entire system failed, with no one taking action for fear it was not what was meant with the instruction: "The most important thing to remember is that you can never put too much water into this nuclear cooling chamber."

The two parties negotiating the lease and those committing the understanding of the negotiation to paper should also remember that during the term other people will have to interpret the intent of the agreement between the two parties.

Poorly negotiated and worded leases increase administrative costs for both the landlord and the tenant. It can lead to account collection problems and poor tenant relations. In the worst case scenarios, it can lead to protracted and expensive legal battles and a significant loss of reputation.

On the other hand, a well-crafted lease should be more than concise and clear, and note the business terms. It should also reflect how the landlord intends to run the property during the term of the lease. It should clearly set expectations and set out the respective obligations on both the landlord and the tenant. For this reason, the landlord should not rely on an 'off the shelf' template lease to meet their needs.

While a landlord 'standard' lease form can serve as the basis for all the landlord's properties, the basic lease form should be modified for the way each property operates.

It is just as inappropriate to use a lease intended for a large, enclosed shopping centre for a grocery anchored open air centre as it is the other way around.

Although many of the property specific matters can be captured in the rules and regulations schedule to the lease or the construction schedule, the entire lease needs to be reviewed with the landlord's objectives for the investment in mind.

Here is a simple example why the lease needs to be tailored to how the property will be operated.

Does the landlord want the tenant to maintain the heating, ventilation and air conditioning system (commonly known as the HVAC system), or will the landlord maintain it at the tenant's cost? Will that landlord-completed maintenance be under a bulk contract covering all the HVAC units at the property, or even over several properties (meaning the landlord may need a basis for apportionment of the costs between properties detailed in the lease), or on an individual store basis?

Conversely, if it has been left to the tenant to maintain, what type of maintenance does the landlord require, how frequent will it be and how will the landlord know the tenant is maintaining the HVAC system?

Then there are the questions of who conducts repairs and replacements beyond regular maintenance of the HVAC system and which party pays for them?

All these questions should be answered in the lease. And you can see that the concept of the transfer of risk is inherent in these questions and answers. As a result, while

HVAC is not a major risk point in the overall lease, the question of who is responsible, and the costs associated with the HVAC system will need to be negotiated as part of the overall negotiation. A lease that doesn't specifically address how the property will be operated will lead to confusion, misunderstanding and the types of issues a good lease is meant to resolve.

Here is a real life example: A landlord in Greater Los Angeles with a multi-tenant office building wanted to save legal costs and used a 'fill-in the blank' type of lease form intended for a single tenant industrial building. Because the lease was for a different asset class it didn't accurately describe the property, what costs should be borne by the tenants and how those costs should be allocated. Because the lease was generic, it didn't account for the particular requirements of the site.

The end results were confusion over the costs, how the property was to operate and each tenant's role in their interactions with other tenants and the landlord as well as lost revenue opportunities, rent collection issues, tenant dissatisfaction, increased management costs and a loss of value and return to the landlord.

A one time saving of a few thousand dollars cost the landlord years of expensive problems.

IN SUMMARY

Investors are more interested in the NOI than the bricks and dirt of real estate.

A change in the net operating income has a compounding affect on the property value. Mistakes are very costly and can carry on for years.

A significant portion of the lease negotiation is about risk transfer between the parties.

A good lease has both a good structure and is well written in clear, concise terms.

Off the shelf leases must be modified to address the operation of the property and how the parties are meant to interact during the term.

Chapter 2
Advanced Lease Negotiating

'Creating a Story to Sell'

In this chapter let's focus on industry specific techniques and processes that allow the landlord to retain as much negotiating position as possible in order to reduce as much risk as possible. Remember, after the basic financial terms are agreed, the balance of the negotiation is all about the transfer of risk from one party to the other. We will also uncover common errors made in negotiating a lease for a retail property and provide specific solutions to those.

There are a number of good books and courses about finding tenants, how to merchandise a centre, etc. There are other good books about general negotiating tactics. Find the ones that work best for you and apply those principles.

Redefining a Retail Property

Redefining how a shopping centre is perceived is perhaps the first and most important step in retaining negotiating power and maximizing the landlord's value equation. We will touch on this concept a few times over the balance of the book.

Interestingly, few people consciously consider what a shopping centre really is; yet, once you understand it, you will immediately see the benefits of thinking of a retail property in a different light.

Wikipedia defines a shopping centre as: "A shopping mall, shopping center/centre, shopping arcade, shopping precinct, or simply mall is one or more buildings forming a complex of shops representing merchandisers, with interconnecting walkways enabling visitors to walk from unit to unit. Other establishments including movie theaters and restaurants are also often included."

The International Council of Shopping Centres (ICSC) has a similar definition and various classifications depending on the size, number of anchor tenants, pedestrian orientation, merchandising mix, etc. For example, there are small neighbourhood centres, Grocery anchored centres, community centres that are either open-air or enclosed, regional and super regional centres, lifestyle centres, power and outlet centres, to name but a few.

There are also retail street corridors and single tenant retail properties, so the classic definition has been expanded to include all these in the broader term of a 'retail property'.

All these various definitions are focused on the physical characteristics such as the land, buildings, number of tenants, etc. What they don't do is consider the essence of what a retail property really is. It is important to the leasing and negotiation process to consider this. It is time to redefine a retail property.

It is more than land and buildings.

It is a distribution channel and provides access to a unique market.

Contemplate this sentence for a minute: "It is a distribution channel and provides access to a unique market." In fact, two adjacent shopping centres can attract two completely different customer segments as a result of their merchandising, massing and focus.

Thinking in marketing terms rather than strictly land and buildings allows the landlord to create a marketing story. We call this creating **A Story To Sell ™**.

Defining a unique market focuses the leasing effort and removes the property from comparable properties. It is no longer the same as all the other properties whether or not those properties have created a unique market focus themselves. The landlord's property is now unique and "incomparable" to the others. If the tenant wants to reach that specific market, that no other property can specifically reach, the tenant is almost required to lease space in that property. As a result, it is possible to obtain above market rents. It isn't simple. To define that unique market that only this one property can access and attract takes time, research and thought, but once done successfully and the landlord can prove that their property is the best way to reach and obtain those customers, the negotiating power remains with the landlord.

Removing the property from a pool of comparable properties is important. Here's why. Comparable products, by definition, are commodities. Gasoline is a prime example. The average consumer believes that the gas they put into their vehicle from one supplier or another is effectively the same. Gas from

Brand "A" is the same as gas from brand "B". It is all gas to run the vehicle. Consumers will literally cross the street to a competing gas station to save a 1/10 of a penny. Once a product or services is defined as a commodity it will result in commodity pricing since there is no discernable difference, advantage or disadvantage between them. The same is true of real estate assets. If there is no difference, there is no marketing story to support the rent pricing or motivation for a tenant to locate their business in your property. When this happens the tenant judges various properties all with the same filter and the tenant holds the negotiating power. In their eyes property "A" and property "B" are the same, so the location they select will come down to the best deal they can negotiate.

Demonstrating that your property has a definable and unique customer base that can only be properly accessed by your property alone separates your property from the masses and allows you to retain negotiating strength.

Examples of this are found everywhere. The landlords on Rodeo Drive in Beverly Hills or on Bloor Street in Toronto command better rents, constant demand for space and better leases, with fewer concessions than a landlord of space just one block away. The same can be said for the owners of Yorkdale Mall in Toronto, the Grove in Los Angeles, Bal Harbor Shops in Florida, Westfield Sydney in Australia and other notable streets and shopping centres.

You may be thinking that holds true for Rodeo Drive, for example, but doesn't really apply to your asset. But it does. Rodeo Drive attracts some of the most luxurious retailers in the world. True it is located in Beverly Hills, a market that can support that type of merchandising, but having that market on the doorstep to Rodeo Drive doesn't automatically result in those two block's unique access to those multi-millionaires. There are several other streets immediately adjacent to Rodeo Drive that don't have the same branding, cache or landlord negotiating strength. They don't have the same unique access.

Now consider the impact on the marketing story of Rodeo Drive if the merchandising moved to discount stores. The same thing can happen with every lease the landlord enters into. Will this tenant, this merchandise, this deal support my story to sell, or detract from it.

Here is a real life example. Grosvenor Americas owns a neighbourhood, grocery anchored shopping centre in British

Columbia. Their *story to sell* is predicated on the property featuring better quality specialty stores. While the property has brand name tenants, the proportion of the specialty stores is greater than average. Even when leasing to food outlets they have defined their strategy simply as "no food outlets with plastic chairs." They actually use this phrase to target their leasing efforts away from the ubiquitous fast food burger and sandwich chains. The asset manager believes that introducing a business with "plastic chairs" will change the character of the property.

Does it work? This property achieves base rents that are comparable to large regional shopping centres in the area, and far above competitor's real estate.

Defining your real estate as a marketing channel with unique access to a market is one of the most important actions an landlord can make in improving their leasing and negotiating power.

Creating a Story to Sell

Creating a unique marketing message is not a simple task, nor should it be glossed over. It is also important that everyone involved in the management, leasing and operation of the property knows, understands and supports the story to sell.

The first step is a critical assessment of the property relative to all potential competitors. This is typically done using a S.W.O.T. analysis.

S.W.O.T. stands for Strengths, Weaknesses, Opportunities and Threats

To complete a SWOT matrix, simply list all the facts under each heading in a matrix similar to the one in the diagram. A SWOT matrix should be completed for the landlord's own asset as well as each competitor. While one sheet can be used for each property, another useful way to do this is to expand each box adding columns for each property and listing each properties' strengths, weaknesses, opportunities and threats side by side.

SWOT Matrix

	HELPFUL (for your objective)	HARMFUL (for your objective)
INTERNAL (within organisation)	**Strengths** • ___ • ___ • ___ • ___ • ___	**Weaknesses** • ___ • ___ • ___ • ___ • ___
EXTERNAL (outside organisation)	**Opportunities** • ___ • ___ • ___ • ___	**Threats** • ___ • ___ • ___ • ___

Strengths and Weaknesses are within the control of the landlord, whereas Opportunities and Threats are typically external and out of the control of the property.

Be as specific as possible when listing each. For example, a strength may be that the property has average sales that are 35% greater than any of the competitors, or the grocery anchor has the largest selection of natural and organic foods in the municipality.

We determined an important strength for one client was that the bank in the property had the highest number of accounts in the trading area valued at over $1million each. This information was weaved into our overall story to sell.

Once the SWOT analysis is completed, determine which strengths are the greatest and most defensible. It is important that the narrative in the story to sell be unique and not easily copied by others.

The third step is to seek a theme from the list of strengths and combine them into a common selling proposition. The individual strengths provide evidence to the story, and more evidence you can provide, the more credibility the story to sell becomes in the mind of prospective tenants.

Ultimately, your story to sell should look something like this:

We serve a unique market because we capture [the most X.Y.Z]. We know this because of [A] and [B] and [C]. We can safely say that no other properties in our trade area can say the same thing. Since this type of market is important to you this is the best, if not the only, location for your business to meet your goals.

The Only Correct Answer in Real Estate

There is only one correct answer in commercial real estate. That answer is:

"It depends."

Every property; every lease transaction; every investor, landlord and tenant is unique and different. Time also plays an important aspect to the answer, as do personal and global economics, politics, risks (both in our control and outside of our control) and a myriad of other factors.

While that answer may sound trite and convenient, it is nevertheless important to remember that every negotiation and lease is unique. This has many implications. Here are just a few:

When negotiating, the tenant may say that other landlords are providing the concession they are requesting or that it is common in the industry. That may be the case, but it does not automatically hold that the concession is valid in this negotiation. An appropriate response is that the tenant wouldn't want to be held to the same conditions other tenants have agreed to, so asking the landlord to base their business decisions around what another landlord will accept is not appropriate. Essentially, the case for the concession *depends* on the specific situation. There is an even better response. That is to use the most effective question in negotiating – which we go over a little later in this section.

If the landlord has uniquely positioned the centre through their story to sell, they can also rely on the argument that other landlords may provide the concession but they aren't accessing that particular market and may need to do that in order to attract a tenant to an inferior location.

Another area when "It depends" is helpful is during the actual lease negotiation. It helps frame a point of reference when used in response to a tenant's requested amendment.

Here is a common example. Too often, the lease is negotiated from the perspective of the current date and situation. However, the lease is an executory document. An executory contract is a **contract** that has not yet been fully performed, that is to say, fully completed or executed. To put it another way, it's a contract under which both sides still have important performance remaining. It is a 'living' contract over the term of the lease.

What may be the case today, may not be the case in six months, or three years from the date of the negotiation. If during the negotiation, the tenant wants an amendment to the lease based upon a circumstance that currently exists, the phrase "It depends, that might change over time," is a great bridge to make a counter point. However, be mindful of the other side of the table using the same thought to obtain concessions such as co-tenancy and restrictive covenant clauses.

When administering to the lease it is also important to remember that each lease is different and a generalized answer will, in most likelihood, not be applicable. Therefore, the best way to determine the correct answer to a question is to look for it in the tenant's specific lease. We call that going to the **'Source Document'**.

It is also critical to remember that the original lease may have been modified over time. All the documents need to be read to avoid a potential leasing mistake. You may find it helpful to start by reading the most recent amendment to the lease and working backward to the original lease document.

Five Criteria for Successful Negotiation

There are five items that determine the success of a negotiation:

1. Experience
2. Aspiration
3. Criteria
4. Trading Value
5. Leverage

Experience

It is important to make a connection with the prospective tenant. It is the experience of the negotiation, not the business terms themselves that will provide satisfaction to the other party. If the prospect feels the negotiation is a bad experience, they will become entrenched in their position or even walk away.

The negotiation is an opportunity to understand their position, needs and objectives. This requires a level of trust and an open experience. It is also an opportunity for the landlord to demonstrate the 'fairness' of their position. That is best done if there is a connection between the parties.

Aspiration

Negotiators who aspire to obtain a higher level achieve it. Studies on negotiating achievers have clearly demonstrated that those who have high aspirations outperform low aspirants irrespective of skill or negotiating power. Throughout this book we provide aspirational positions for this very reason. You may not achieve all of them in a particular negotiation; but the combination of the positions naturally raises the bar.

Criteria

What does success look like? What is the benchmark used <u>going into the negotiation</u>? There have been many scholarly books on benchmarking, so they won't be repeated here. However, the points that apply here are the following:

- The benchmark should be set to the ideal outcome. Since 1927, the baseball home run King was Babe Ruth, who had hit .356 that year and smashed 60 homers out over fences measuring up to 450 feet in dead center. Babe Ruth never approached the plate with the anticipation of just hitting a single. It was always with the intention of hitting a home run. His ideal outcome. That was his benchmark.

- Look outside the established parameters in setting the benchmark. Southwest Airlines studied NASCAR pit crews to speed up terminal turnarounds – not other airlines.

Trading Value

The essence of all contracts is an exchange of value. Each party provides something in exchange for something else. It is important during the negotiation to uncover what is of value to the prospective tenant. All value is subjective. This means that what is valuable to one person at one time may not be valuable to another person or to the same person at a different time. Therefore it is important to demonstrate the value of your offering after uncovering what is of value to the prospect.

There is a fundamental psychological difference between "price", "cost" and "value". The definition of price is: *the amount required as payment for something offered for sale.*

The definition of cost is: *an amount that has to be paid or spent to obtain something.*

The definition of value is: *considered (someone or something) to be important or beneficial.*

Price and cost are inverses of each other and are at either end of the spectrum. Cost is what the buyer parts with. An inherently negative emotion is associated with the word and concept of "cost" as the buyer is parting with something they already value, typically money. Some associate "cost" with "loss". Price is what the seller obtains. Perceived value is the negotiating band between the two. The more value imparted for the cost, the higher the price the buyer is willing to pay and the more the buyer is willing to complete the transaction. Bear in mind that the buyer needs to obtain something they perceive more valuable than what they are parting with. Therefore, to obtain maximum price the buyer must receive the perceived maximum value. The more value, the less the buyer thinks of "cost" and the more they think of what is being obtained. Think of a speedometer to remember this.

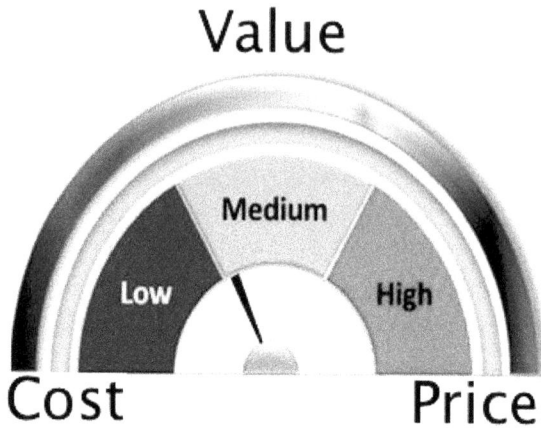

Value

Medium

Low　High

Cost　　　　　**Price**

This reinforces the concept of the commoditization of real estate. The term *commodity* is used to describe a class of goods for which there is demand, but which is supplied without a qualitative differentiation across a market. For example, wheat is a commodity. The market doesn't care who produced it, and arguably, there is little quality differentiation. There is little value differentiation. Without a Story to Sell and a constant reinforcement of the value the retailer receives in completing the transaction, one retail property may look the same as the next, so the retailer will consider cost as the primary differentiation and negotiate on the basis of cost. The landlord needs to constantly reference the value of the property and the transaction to the retailer in order to get the best price.

Leverage

Leverage is obtained by uncovering value and providing that value. It is also gained by providing something that can only be obtained from one source, but unless that unique something is considered valuable by the other party, then a transaction can't be completed.

Maintaining leverage during the negotiation means constantly checking what is valuable to the prospect, using active listening techniques, and reinforcing your message of a unique and special offering.

One of the most important tools in keeping leverage is the appropriate use of the word "No". However, ever since we were all very young we have learned that "NO" induces some form of trauma. Therefore, there are two important rules to using this tool:

1. Know when to say "No". This comes from setting the negotiating priorities and knowing what is important to you as an outcome of the transaction. In other words, knowing the criteria for success.
2. Know how to say "No". There are ways to provide a positive "No". Two of the more effective ways are:

a. Provide an alternative. Essentially, you are saying "We aren't able to do that now, but we can provide this."
b. Offer an explanation for not being able to do something. This may mollify their request or open the door to an alternative.

You should keep in mind with the first option that you are pre-supposing a concession to your position unless you also obtain some other concession from the prospect in the process. The dialogue goes along the line of this: "Unfortunately, as it sits right now, we can't accommodate that; however, if we revisit ABC, then we can provide XYZ."

Notice how the leverage is maintained because the prospect must give up something else to obtain their request or some portion of it. Throughout the book we offer suggestions of *Quid Pro Quo* alternatives.

Ultimately, there must still be a decisive "No" retained in the landlord's negotiating toolbox. There has never been a good outcome from a bad transaction. The landlord must know when - and be able - to walk away from a bad lease negotiation. But even then, the landlord should retain the relationship and end the experience on as positive a note as possible.

When the landlord must walk away from the negotiating table, it is best to explain that it isn't in either party's interest to continue the negotiation as is stands and invite the prospect to return to the discussion if they can see a way to an acceptable solution. The landlord still retains leverage should the prospect return to the negotiation with a modified position.

The Only Question You Really Need in Negotiation

Since the negotiation is a meeting of the minds about the basic business terms and acceptable risks assumed by both parties, it is important to truly understand what is most important to the tenant and to understand their frame of reference.

The easiest way is to simply ask the question "Why?"

"Why?" is an open ended question intended to expose the reasoning behind the request.

Obviously, if you repeated "Why?" to every request and comment, it would sound silly, if not idiotic. Fortunately there are a number of ways to ask the question:

"Why is that important?"

"Can you help me understand the significance of this request?"

"What is the context for this?"

"What is the background to this request?"

"When has this been important to you?"

And many other phrases.

Just keeping the question of "Why?" alive in the back of your mind alerts you to potential issues and alternatives.

Here are two examples of the power of the question of "Why?" that are covered in a later chapter.

Example #1

Tenant: "I need three, five year options to renew my lease."

Landlord: "Why do you want those?"

Tenant: "I don't want to build up my business and have my space at risk."

The take away is the tenant may not need to have the lease renewed so much as an assurance of having the ability to retain his space for the longer term.

Example #2

Tenant: "I want a mutual indemnity clause in the lease."

Landlord: "Why is that important?"

Tenant: "You are asking me to indemnify you, and I pay the insurance premiums as part of my CAM that you take out, so I want you to be covered under the insurance first and not just come to me."

The take away is that the tenant doesn't understand how the insurance and indemnity provisions work so a step-down to the standard clause may be more appropriate than adding a Landlord indemnity.

Some professional lease wording negotiators send the tenant their standard lease form and ask the tenant to provide their top X number of issues. The number X varies between 3 to 7. The intent of this tactic is to boil down the discussion to the most meaningful points for both the tenant and the landlord. They then use the "Why?" technique on those burning issues.

Avoid These 10 Common Lease Negotiating Errors

Since every negotiation is unique, it is important to review the negotiation at its end to learn from the experience. Expert lease negotiators do this after every transaction and make notes for subsequent negotiations. Here are some of the most frequent errors to occur during the negotiation:

1. Not understanding the impact of any concessions on the balance of the property in terms of subsequent leasing, added costs, added management time, added risk, cost to value, etc.

    It is acceptable to work out the math before making a commitment to any concession.

2. A similar error is not cross-checking the impact of a concession against other aspects of the lease wording under negotiation and any modifications to those clauses.

3. A common error is to make an assumption based on generalizations and common sense. In this case common sense is the belief that the knowledge or practice is common and universal. Remember "It Depends" is the only right answer in real estate.

Here is a real world example of these first three errors compounding to such an extent that the landlord lost their entire multi-million dollar investment in foreclosure.

The landlord developed a small two building property. Each building was leased to sophisticated brand name chains.

One tenant modified the standard lease clause pertaining to the payment of property tax so that the tenant would pay directly to the taxing authority any taxes that were separately assessed and billed to the tenant and failing such a separate assessment and billing, the taxes would be billed as part of common area maintenance (CAM).

The landlord felt that on the face of the wording this was an acceptable amendment to the clause, confident in how the taxes were assessed and billed since that is how it was done on his last project in another city.

His 'common sense' guided him as he had
seen it done this way before.

Unfortunately, this municipality only
assessed and billed property taxes to the lot
owner and only on the singular lot and not
the individual tenants. The tenant refused to
pay the tax bill the landlord presented, as it
was not in accordance with the lease.
Therefore, the landlord had to rely on
collecting the taxes due via CAM. However,
when agreeing to the CAM clause the
landlord also agreed to a limit, or cap, on the
tenant's contribution to those expenses and
that cap was based on the limited scope of
expenses anticipated as common area
maintenance exclusive of the tax. The math
during negotiation didn't include the
possibility of taxes being billed as part of
CAM.

Since the CAM cap barely covered the actual
common maintenance costs, and the tenant
lived to the letter of the lease there was a
shortfall equal to the tenant's entire portion
of the taxes (roughly 50% of the total tax
bill). The landlord had to bear that portion
of the taxes itself, with the funds coming
from the minimum rent the tenant paid.

The resulting tax burden was so
cumbersome that the landlord was unable to

maintain its other obligations and the property went into foreclosure.

All three of the above errors played out with dramatic and unfortunate results that cost the landlord millions of dollars. The entire issue could have been avoided by:

- not relying on 'common sense', but checking how the taxes were assessed and billed,
- cross checking the tax clause to the CAM clause, and
- recognizing a potential issue (even without checking how the taxes were done) and changing the CAM wording to exclude taxes from the cap.

This landlord also didn't know how to correct the problem.

When we acquired the asset, we spent a few thousand dollars to subdivide the property. It was a fraction of the annual cost the landlord had to bear. The subdivision allowed the taxing authority to separately assess and bill the taxes to the tenant's personal account. Problem solved.

4. Not recognizing that the lease is executory and "live" for the lease term, as we previously discussed.

5. Not knowing what risks are unacceptable. Every landlord should have a concise list of deal breakers and be prepared to walk away from the negotiation if needed. Remember that mistakes in real estate can haunt you for a very long time and can be expensive to unwind.

6. Not having a series of standard step-downs to important clauses. A step-down is a modification to the existing language that is acceptable to the landlord. For example, if the lease wording is that a tenant must cure a non-monetary breach of the lease within 15 days and the tenant asks for 30 days the negotiator should know if that step-down is acceptable and under which circumstances 30 days may be too long (Hint: any situation that creates a risk to life, property, insurance coverage or title to the property should have immediate cure provisions written into the modified clause - notwithstanding that they are non-monetary defaults).

7. Negotiating clauses in isolation. This typically occurs when the lease is negotiated on a 'page turn' basis. In this type of negotiation each clause is reviewed and negotiated in the order they appear in the lease, one page after the other.

When using this negotiation style is it more difficult to remember what was previously conceded, as our hapless developer/landlord found in the example above.

This type of negotiation also can result in more modifications to the lease than the landlord intended as each change, in and of itself, doesn't seem to be significant. Even if it is a significant change, the impact can go un-noticed. An example of this is when a tenant asks for a construction allowance or for the landlord to complete some work in the premises near the end of the negotiation. This is done long after the initial rent terms have been agreed to, but it has a direct bearing on the financial performance of that lease.

8. Not recognizing the interdependence of certain business terms in the lease. Failing to recognize and use those moments hurts the landlord's negotiating position.

   Here is how it works. The tenant asks for an exclusivity clause in the lease. Why do they want that? (There's that "why" question again). Because the tenant wants to protect and maximize their sales. The quid pro quo to an exclusivity clause is percentage rent. If the tenant truly desires an exclusivity right to protect their sales, then the landlord has every right to negotiate a percentage rent clause as compensation for that clause.

   The landlord has now given the tenant an either/or option in the negotiation. Assuming that the exclusivity is not a deal breaker for the landlord, they retain their negotiating power. The tenant must now decide if the exclusivity is worth the possibility of paying percentage rent, or to forego the exclusivity to avoid percentage rent.

9. Using a precedent lease form. A tenant will want to use a precedent lease form if the lease is more favorable to their

position. Precedent leases tend to be on the tenant's lease document or are so highly modified from the landlord's original lease that they mirror a tenant's own lease. The landlord's lease should reflect how the landlord wants to operate the property, so precedent lease forms should be avoided.

Agreeing to use clause step-down wording that was agreed to in the past between the landlord and the tenant should be fine and can expedite the overall negotiation. The use of previously agreed step-downs still requires a review of the present situation, because the negotiating strength of the parties may change over time and some of the concessions previously granted may no longer apply.

Here is a real life, egregious example of the improper use of a precedent lease form.

A third party agent representing the landlord wrote an offer to lease agreeing to use another landlord's precedent lease document for the prospective tenant. You can probably see that there are a number of issues with this approach.

The landlord wanting to complete a deal with this tenant has no idea what the other landlord conceded in the lease. The current landlord has no idea how strong the negotiating strength of the parties were at the time of the other lease. The precedent concessions may put the landlord offside with their own landlord's insurance company or mortgage conditions, so they need to be vetted and not blindly agreed to. And obtaining another landlord's lease for review may be difficult, so the current landlord would have to take the concessions on face value and believe they came from a single lease rather than an amalgamation of many favorable terms of various leases.

It also must call into question the alliance of the agent with the landlord.

10.   Not considering subsequent leasing decisions in every lease negotiation. This is related to the first error but is broader in scope. This error pertains to leasing decisions related to the tenant in question, and their specific lease, as well as other

leases in the property. Unfortunately, this error is all too common. The landlord looks at the lease on an individual basis rather than part of a larger picture. Here are just a few potential outcomes:

- Too many and broadly worded exclusivities or co-tenancy clauses compound to hamper other leasing efforts.
- Demising a space into an "L" shaped configuration can land lock part of the rentable area, making it unleasable in the future.
- Recoverable expense concessions such as a cap on contributions can hurt future profit.
- Chasing the immediate opportunity and leasing to the wrong merchant/use that can affect the public and other tenant's perception of the property; resulting in a loss of traffic and problems leasing.

These 10 are some of the most common, general errors in negotiating lease terms. Avoiding these will result in better leases with less risk to the landlord. Specific clauses and the impact of the negotiation are covered in Parts 2 and 3 of the book.

Aspirational Bonus Point

It is always easier to remove a negotiating point than to introduce one. Our customizable lease template is over 50 pages in length. The lease is that long for two reasons.

1. Unfortunately, it just needs to be that long to capture all the legal requirements, and
2. Experience is a great teacher and as issues have been encountered in the past, they have been resolved with additional clarification in the lease.

A lease should never contain clauses specifically used as throw away negotiating points. However, it is easier to negotiate when all the points of the negotiation are presented up front, so the lease should be written as the 'best case' outcome for the landlord.

IN SUMMARY

It is important to make your property 'incomparable' by defining it as a unique marketing and distribution channel to a desirable market that property alone can deliver. Then create a Story to Sell™

There is no one-size-fits-all correct answer in commercial real estate and commercial real estate leasing. The correct answer is "It Depends."

Negotiating strength is retained when the landlord understands the underlying rationale for the tenant's position on any negotiating point. One question is most effective in getting that understanding.

There are at least 10 common errors made in negotiating a lease. These were reviewed in this chapter.

Chapter 3
Advisors and More

The way a team plays as a whole determines its success. You may have the greatest bunch of individual stars in the world, but if they don't play together, the club won't be worth a dime.

Babe Ruth

There are three third party professionals who should never negotiate the lease on the landlord's behalf. Those are: a real estate agent or broker, a lawyer and an accountant. Here is why.

The Real Estate Agent

Negotiating the lease is not why a landlord engages a third party real estate agent, nor is it the best use of their time, energy and expertise.

The agent, or broker as they are also called by some even though those are separate functions, primary value is in providing market intelligence, including finding suitable prospects for your vacant space.

A good real estate agent should be a specialist in the retail asset class and preferably in the specific subclass. This specialization permits them to know all that is happening in the geographic market of the property. If they are with a large brokerage firm, the firm may also have a local research department that can be used to obtain a breadth of information concerning general market conditions including comparable rent structures, new developments planned or underway and prospect tenant activity as well as general economic and political market conditions.

The wise landlord avails themselves of this information; and determining what the agent knows and how they obtained that knowledge should be key questions in the listing interview process. The listing process is reviewed in greater detail a little later.

The ability to source new tenants is partially based on the general market knowledge of both the agent and the agency they represent. This is the primary reason for using an agent.

The agent's most valuable role is to find a suitable prospect and have them commit to the basic business terms for a lease, as outlined in the landlord's standard offer form or letter of intent. Thereafter the agent should be focused on securing the next new prospect, not negotiating the fine points of the lease. That should be the responsibility of the landlord or one of their key internal roles.

There are two simple reasons for this.

First and foremost is that the lease represents the business arrangement between the landlord and the tenant. The third party agent, by definition, is not a party to the ongoing relationship and daily operation of the lease. It is important that the landlord build the business relationship and understanding of the way the tenant and landlord interact from the very start of the negotiations. This process ensures clarity and removes the possibility of the tenant saying the agent promised something or lead the tenant to believe something later in the lease term.

The second reason is that the landlord and their management representatives can provide operational insight into the lease negotiation itself. This can speed the negotiation process because there are fewer people involved and fewer channels of communication. It can also eliminate costly errors.

Here is a real life example. The prospect wanted an identification sign on the property's pylon sign and the real estate agent, who was charged with negotiating the entire lease, readily agreed since the negotiations were coming to a close and this was one of the last items in the back and forth negotiation of the lease. Unfortunately, this property didn't have a pylon sign. After the lease was signed by the tenant, and the landlord told them there was no pylon sign, the tenant felt the landlord's leasing agent dealt in bad faith.

Obviously, the situation could have been avoided had the agent contacted the landlord about a sign possibility before agreeing to it with the prospect. However, the better solution is for the landlord to always conduct the detailed lease negotiation after the letter of intent or the offer to lease has been signed.

The Lawyer

Every landlord should have (on speed dial) a highly skilled and experienced lawyer who is a specialist in commercial lease law. That doesn't mean the lawyer should conduct the actual lease negotiation for many of the same reasons the real estate agent shouldn't negotiate the fine points of the lease either.

The primary value of a lawyer is to mitigate the landlord's risk. While negotiation is all about risk transfer from one party to another, it is also all about the way the property is to operate. Moreover, only the landlord should decide on the amount of risk tolerance they can accept as they are the most versed in the larger picture of their investment(s). Conversely, the lawyer should be primarily concerned about this specific contract and the impact of legislation on the contract.

The Accountant

The landlord's accountant typically doesn't possess the real estate skill set to negotiate items such as use clauses, radius restrictions, tenant build-out requirements, insurance requirements, etc. And rightly so. Their highest value is more aligned to the basic business terms of rent and term. The accountant can advise the landlord on how accretive the deal is to the overall financial objectives of the property.

It Takes a Team

No one professional, including the landlord, should be solely charged with concluding a lease negotiation, though all should know all aspects of the lease and the negotiation.

Each of the agent, lawyer and accountant should take direction and also advise their client – the landlord; but, the responsibility for a great lease rests exclusively with the landlord.

Likewise, the landlord must obtain, and take, the advice of their advisors internally and externally. So while no single person should be involved in the negotiation and drafting of the lease, a robust team of industry specialists should be cultivated.

The same applies to the tenant's side of the negotiation. The landlord should negotiate directly with the decision maker for the tenant rather than their lawyer or accountant. The landlord should always respect the agency arrangement between the tenant and their agent (if applicable) and request that the landlord conduct final negotiations with the agent's client directly.

Again, the obvious reason is to establish that business relationship and set expectations as early as possible.

The landlord may also find that the tenant is receiving advice from people who are not specialists in commercial real estate and retail properties. For example, the tenant may engage a lawyer who is not well versed in the concepts of percentage rent. This can slow, stall or even terminate a negotiation. The best way to handle this situation is to have a conversation directly with the tenant, telling them that ultimately the landlord will be dealing with the tenant and not their lawyer on a day to day basis.

Depending on the situation, the landlord may also have the landlord's agent, lawyer or accountant speak with their opposite on the tenant's side of the table.

Here is a real life example. A tenant's lawyer (who was not a specialist in commercial leases) called after they received the lease. His opening statement was that the landlord's lease was 'Draconian' and he was going to advise his client not to sign it, killing the deal. The solution was to call the tenant to ask if they wanted the space in the property to which they said 'yes!' The tenant was told what the lawyer had said about not signing the lease, which was the lawyer's attempt to gain negotiating leverage. The tenant fired the lawyer, obtained a specialist lawyer and the transaction was completed within a week.

The Listing Agreement

Here are a few tips when using third party real estate agents and their listing agreements.

Listing agreements are commonly exclusive arrangements so the landlord can't engage multiple brokerages. The reason being that the agent will incur costs in developing marketing materials. We feel at the very least, the arrangement should carve out any transactions secured independently by the landlord.

The listing agreement should always be time limited with termination provisions for non-performance. There shouldn't be any automatic renewal provisions.

The agreement should spell out exactly what the agent will do to market the property, such as the number of calls or meetings that will be made exclusively regarding your asset, how many brochures will be mailed to a prospect list and which prospects are targeted. If it is a large brokerage, how will the landlord's property be promoted internally? The landlord must have approval rights over all marketing material created for the property.

The landlord should get all promises and commitments made during the listing pitch incorporated into the listing agreement. The agent should be held accountable to their promises and they need to report regularly to the landlord. Once a month is not too many times. If the agent doesn't report in written form, then the landlord should take detailed notes about the meeting in case there are performance issues.

The agent should only use the offer or letter of intent provided by the landlord so the important terms of the landlord's unique lease are captured.

While the agent will want to secure rights to all renewal leasing, the landlord should avoid this. The reason is that the agent may not have had a daily relationship with the tenant between first introducing them to the property and the time of the renewal. The landlord has had that relationship over 5 to 10 years, so the tenant's desire to renew is based on that relationship and the broker has not added significant value to the relationship at that point. The agent should be focused only on securing a steady stream of new prospects for the property.

The landlord should expect to pay fair market commissions to the agent. The landlord should recognize that third party agents are self employed and 100% commissioned based in their compensation, in most instances. Therefore, reducing their commission structure below market may result in the agent paying more attention to higher paying assignments. Remember they are in business too and their inventory are their listings.

The listing agreement should carve out any prospects the landlord is in active negotiations with at the time of the listing. Also expect that the agent will create a reserve list of their active prospects for commissions payable when their listing is cancelled. This is another reason for regular reporting and a performance clause in the agreement. Only those tenants the agent has reported as in active negotiation should be on the reserve list. The agent shouldn't be able to reserve any tenants as a result of termination due to non-performance.

IN SUMMARY

The landlord is solely responsible to ensure a great lease is negotiated, but should assemble and consult with a team of advisors during the negotiation process.

The landlord should select lawyers, accountant and agents who are specialists in commercial real estate and in retail properties.

Beware the real estate agent's standard listing agreement. It should be as vigorously negotiated as any lease.

Chapter 4
Negotiating Basic Rent

Comparable rent will never maximize the rent of an incomparable property.

Basic Rent is also referred to as Minimum Rent, Net Rent or Base Rent by many people. It is the third leg of the rental stool, with the other two being Additional Rent and Percentage Rent, both of which are covered in other chapters.

How Basic Rent is determined and negotiated should be different depending on the answers to the following questions:

- Is this a new development property, or an existing stabilized asset?
- Was this space previously under negotiation with this or another prospect?

- Is this a renewal of an existing tenancy?

An obvious fourth question would be: What is the budget? However, negotiating to budget is not aspirational.

Basic rent is intended to cover the landlord's fixed costs of the real estate and to produce a profit acceptable to the landlord. This stands repeating:

Basic rent must cover the landlord's fixed costs of the real estate and to produce a profit acceptable to the landlord.

While this sound elementary, the concept behind this statement appears to be lost on those who negotiate based on comparable properties. Note that everything in the definition is personal to the individual property and the individual landlord. Therefore, while comparing various assets does provide a benchmark range, negotiating based only on what other landlords are charging for their assets (ie: negotiating based on comps alone) negates the individuality of the property and the landlord needs. It negates the Story to Sell.

In this chapter we build on the concept of the Story to Sell and how to negotiate for the maximum rental value.

Determining the Minimum Rent for a New Development.

In its simplest form, determining the Basic Rent for a new development is essentially a mathematical calculation obtained by dividing the total development costs incurred plus the anticipated return on the investment by the rentable area.

In truth, there are a lot of variables to be considered. Some of these include:

- the type of development (ie: stand alone retail, shopping centre or a portion of a mixed use development);
- the exit strategy being either a long term hold or an immediate sale once stabilized;
- the nature of the development as a single block or a phased development; and,
- comparable market rents.

Notwithstanding the previous comment concerning the individuality of the property, development properties are more susceptible to comparable pricing as they do not have an established performance history to set them apart, so new developments lack a critical statement of proof. However, the Story to Sell for a new development can focus on the intended market, the other tenant's reasons for leasing in the property, etc.

Given the many variables involved in new developments, the pricing of rent must be taken in context of the entire development process. Whole books concerning real estate development practices exist so we won't duplicate all that information here. Instead the focus will be on negotiating rent for existing assets.

However, the landlord should know the cost of new developments in the area of the landlord's property, as this too comprises part of the comparable range of market rents the landlord needs to understand.

Setting Basic Rent for Vacant Space

One of the most common ways to price space, as noted before, is to compare the rent to other properties. Additionally, many leasing agents and landlords set a uniform rental rate across the rentable area of the property.

There are several issues with these approaches if the landlord wants to maximize the rental income.

Using only comparable rents negates the individuality of the asset and its strengths compared to those other properties. Essentially, the landlord who relies only on comparable rent is adopting the strengths and weaknesses of those other assets. And in the context of negotiating the rent, it will be the weaknesses that will be highlighted. Likewise, having a single rate throughout the property irrespective of size, frontage, position and merchandising, negates all these factors in the landlord's property.

To maximize the rent in negotiation, the landlord must have a simple Story to Sell. The landlord also needs to have proof that what they are telling the prospective tenant is true.

One of the key ways to both sell the property and provide proof is the sales performance of the centre and/or like merchants, without impinging on the other tenant's privacy and confidentiality. The merchant is looking for a location that will produce the maximum sales for their enterprise. Knowledgeable retailers have large databases and can predict their performance based on the market information, including the performance of the centre.

Many landlords of smaller properties don't collect sales data. The expert landlord creates a competitive advantage simply by having the sales information at hand.

Here is a sample negotiating script that positions the landlord's property favorably:

Landlord: "You are seeking a location that allows you to produce maximum sales, right?"

Prospect: "Yes."

Landlord: "With our property we provide you with actual average sales information; albeit because it is an average some will produce more sales than stated, while others will have less. Now lets compare that to other properties in the area. Many don't even know what the sales performance of their site is. If you want to maximize sales, don't you want to know if the property is capable of meeting your sales needs? If you don't have another property's sales information, you are missing important key data that determines your sales and if the rent is reasonable."

Used in conjunction with the Story to Sell, the following method has been used to achieve base rents as much as 35% above market.

The premise of the method is that the total occupancy costs for the property will make up about 1/3 (or less) of the aggregate of the basic rent and CAM occupancy costs. Equally important is the number of 15%. The total of base rent and CAM occupancy costs should not be more than 15% of sales. Please note the phrase "CAM occupancy costs" because the calculation excludes the tenant services charge noted in Chapter 6.

As a result of these calculations, the basic rent should be 10% of the sales if the CAM occupancy charges make up a further 5% of sales.

But what sales number should be used?

The answer is the <u>greater of</u> the tenant's anticipated third year of sales, the current annual average sales for the centre and, if the centre has existing stores in the same merchandising category as the prospect, the category average sales. Here is why.

The landlord should always seek tenants that enhance the average sales productivity of the merchandise category or the centre; unless some special mitigating circumstance exists or the tenant is truly in a business where sales information cannot be obtained, such as a bank. The ever-increasing sales performance demonstrates market capture. In addition, each new tenant that has sales greater than the average, raises the average.

The landlord wants the tenant's anticipated third year sales for a few reasons. The most important are:

- it weeds out tenants who would actually reduce the centre average or who cannot maximize the rent because

their cost of rent would be too great for
them to be successful,
- the sales information can be tied to
  other clauses in the lease negotiation
  such as a condition to exercise an
  option to renew,
- the third year represents a more
  stabilized sales expectation than the
  first year ramp up or the second year
  (which can actually be lower than the
  first year sales for some initially
  popular stores).

The tenant's sales projection is compared to
the centre's average sales for the reason
noted. In some cases the tenant's use will
create sales less than the average. For
example, a dry-cleaning depot should have
less sales volume than a full service, sit-
down restaurant or a jeweler; but they
produce good frequent trip generation and
may be a desired use.

If the prospect is still desired, even if their
projected sales volume is below the centre
average, the landlord should use the centre's
average sales rather than the tenant's
projection otherwise the landlord is
effectively discounting its (limited) inventory.

However, the landlord needs to be careful
concerning the total cost of the rent to the
tenant's relative sales volume. If it is too

high, it may indicate that the either the prospect is not appropriate and another tenant within the same category should be entertained, or the centre cannot afford the particular use category.

If the centre is large enough to host several tenants within the same merchandising category, then the average sales of that category should be used if it is greater than the centre average because, some categories produce more sales than others. The landlord would again be discounting its space if this was not considered.

The landlord now has up to three base rent options in hand to negotiate; but, a fourth metric also needs to be considered. The rents arrived at from the above math should be considered against the highest and the most recent rents achieved for comparable space in the landlord's own property. An internal, same property rent comparison is appropriate because it is a true "like case" comparison verses comparing rents at different properties.

Now the art of leasing and lease negotiation comes into play. With all the various rent objectives now known, the landlord needs to determine the rent structure that is the optimum to conclude a deal. It may not be the highest rent of the options presented;

however this method should continually produce increasing rents overall and better rents than basing the property's rent strictly against other properties.

The base rent should be increased periodically during the term as well. At a minimum the base rent at the end of the term should at least equal the rate of inflation over the term to maintain the value of the asset. One reason for doing this is that it is easier to obtain further rent increments as the tenant is renewed as compared to one large increase as each term expires. Basic human nature dictates that the tenant will recoil and negotiate harder at what seems to be a single large increase.

Although the tenant is asked to provide the anticipated third year sales, the answer is used to determine the first year of basic rent. For example, if the tenant indicates that their anticipated third years sales volume would be $300.00 per square foot, then the Basic Rent should start at $30.00 per square foot per annum.

These methods establish the minimum rent for the prospect exclusive of inducements, which need to be factored into the rent as an add-on. The incentives should also include a rate of return to the landlord in addition to the actual cost.

This too gives the Landlord negotiating leverage as the prospect is presented with various rent options. To illustrate how this might work, lets assume the landlord and tenant have agreed to a 5 year term with the following Basic Rent structure:

Two years at $20.00 per square foot per annum

One year at $22.00 per square foot per annum, and

Two years at $24.00 per square foot per annum.

The tenant then asks for a leasehold improvement incentive and free rent that equals a total of $20.00 per square foot; or, stated differently, $4.00 per square foot per annum over the term of the lease.

Assuming that the landlord is agreeable to the amount and the landlord's overall return on this property is 10%, the landlord can counter with adding $4.40 to basic rent in each year of the term.

The tenant then is presented with the rent as originally agreed and no incentives, or the higher rent with the incentive.

Incentives will be dealt with in greater detail shortly; but for now let's address basic rent during a renewal.

Setting Basic Rent for a Renewal of a Tenant

Although renewal clauses are addressed further in Chapter 7, the basic rent for the renewal period ties into the negotiation of the basic rent for the initial term. The landlord should always attempt to refrain from negotiating a structured rent during the renewal period, opting instead for a formula. A structured rent specifies the amount of rent for the renewal periods.

There are differences in negotiating rent for a renewal term as compared to the first lease with a tenant. To start, the landlord should have obtained sales information from the commencement of the lease. This allows the landlord to mine actual data as compared to tenant projections.

Ideally, the landlord may have also received percentage rent during the initial term. This adds another data point to the four previously noted because the aggregate of the previous basic rent and percentage rent should be converted into a new basic rent 'floor' during the negotiation. The landlord should always attempt to negotiate above that floor, using the technique used for a vacant space.

It is important that the landlord again consider the 'greater of' the sales projection, a trending line based on the sales history, the aggregate of the basic rent and percentage rent paid (if any), the average sales of the category (if applicable), the average sales of the centre and the highest and most recent rent achieved in the centre.

A Word about Rates of Inflation

A rate of inflation clause can be added to a Basic Rent structure during the initial term but is more common as part of a formula for setting the Basic Rent for a renewal.

Typically, the index used to determine inflation is the Consumer Price Index (also known as the CPI) published by the government. The CPI measures the change in the price of a common and mostly stable basket of consumer goods, such as groceries, fuel, utilities, etc.

Therein lies an issue for commercial landlords. The CPI, while almost universally accepted by landlords and tenants, measures the inflation of the wrong thing. It does not measure the pricing difference of real estate over time, which can be – and has historically proven to be – very different than, say, the price of a loaf of bread over time. CPI does not measure the factors that lead to increases in the price of commercial real estate.

The change in price of commercial real estate is predicated on a multitude of different items unrelated to just consumer products; including, the cost of new construction, the cost of capital, the price of other investments and consumer inflation. Therefore, a different metric is needed to gauge the change in the pricing of commercial real estate over time.

That metric is the percentage change in the appraised value of the property over a period of time. Since the appraised value compares the property to other real estate it takes into consideration the many other factors beyond a basket of consumer goods yet keeps it within the commercial real estate industry. It is a metric that is easily defended in a negotiation as being the true indicator of inflation within the commercial real estate industry.

Incentives

The cost of incentives should be calculated into the overall transaction whether included in the Basic Rent, as a credit to Percent Rent or repaid separately as part of the Additional Rent.

Since the incentive equates to alternate financing in many cases, an interest factor should be added as well. The amount of interest is dependent on the landlord's needs and requirements; but as a rule of thumb it should not be less than the yield on the NOI of the property as determined by the most recent appraisal or the landlord's weighted average cost of capital, whichever is greater.

In negotiating the type of incentive, the Landlord should always ensure that there are repayment mechanisms built into the clause, or elsewhere in the lease, in case of a default by the tenant, or any other type of non-performance, such as a rent relief program. After all, the incentive was originally agreed in consideration of the full performance of the lease.

If the landlord is providing any type of incentive, including a period of free rent, then the tenant must meet certain conditions before receiving it. These should include:

(a) The Tenant has completed the Premises for occupancy in accordance with the Tenant's obligations and the Tenant drawings approved by the Landlord;

(b) The Tenant has secured and submitted to the Landlord all applicable inspection, completion and occupancy certificates for the Premises and the Tenant, and its contractors and sub-contractors have complied with all statutory provisions respecting Builders' Liens and/or Mechanics' Liens, statutory trusts and holdbacks (if any), and the applicable holdback periods have expired without any liens or other claims being filed;

(c) The Tenant has provided the Landlord with a Statutory Declaration stating that there are no Builders' Liens, Workman's Compensation Liens or other liens or encumbrances affecting the Premises or the Shopping Centre in respect to work, services, materials and equipment relating to the Premises and that the Tenant's designers, contractors, sub-contractors, workmen and suppliers of materials and equipment (if any) have been paid in full for all work and services performed and materials and equipment supplied by them on or to the Premises;

(d) The Tenant has executed and returned the Lease to the Landlord in a form acceptable to the Landlord. The Covenantor's Agreement, if applicable, executed by the Covenantor and returned to the Landlord;

(e) Receipt by the Landlord from the Tenant of a written notice requesting payment of the incentive – if it is a monetary incentive such as a construction loan or allowance- together with evidence satisfactory to the Landlord of the actual out-of-pocket costs incurred and paid by the Tenant for the Tenant's Work;

(f) The Tenant has supplied duly executed copies of all documents as required by the Landlord's mortgagee, debenture holders and Trustees under trust deeds; and

(g)   The Tenant has provided copies of their operating insurance to the Landlord.

If the incentive is a period of free rent, it should be negotiated to start after the lien period (if any) has expired. This can be as long as 55 days or more, so the free rent should start in the third month of the term.

If the free rent is more than one month, the negotiation should attempt to spread out the periods over different lease years. For example, the landlord may negotiate three months of basic rent free as part of the transaction. This may be spread out as one month in the first three years of the term or one month in the first, third and fifth year of the term, or some other combination. The purpose of this is that the landlord's risk is mitigated should the tenant not complete the lease.

IN SUMMARY

Setting Basic Rent strictly by using comparable rent from other properties will not maximize the rent opportunity.

There is a four-step process to determining the rent before the negotiation.

Obtaining sales information from existing and prospective tenants is vital to enhancing the negotiating position of the landlord.

The Consumer Price Index is the wrong metric for Base Rent escalators. There is a better method for determining inflation in commercial real estate.

Incentives, if required should be added to the rent, attract an interest component to the landlord and should be recaptured by the landlord in case of non-performance by the tenant.

Chapter 5
Getting Percentage Rent

'Percentage Rent is one of the most under used negotiating tools'

Percentage rent – also called Sales Rent, Override Rent, and/or Overage Rent – is a concept unique to retail properties. It is not found in office or industrial leases. Since it is limited to this one asset class of commercial real estate it is perhaps one of the most misunderstood lease concepts. It is misunderstood as to its intent and function in a lease, when it should and shouldn't be applied, how important it is to the overall negotiation and the math behind it.

It has been called "a cure for the landlord's mistake in setting basic, or minimum rent," "onerous on the tenant," " a dollar grab by greedy landlords;" and worse.

After the year 2000 it has fallen out of practice in most retail properties except regional malls, but it shouldn't be discounted. It is one of the most important tools in the landlord's leasing toolbox, when used in context.

The Intent and Function

Percentage rent is a form of rent that is in addition to the minimum rent and the recovery of operating expenses. Later in this chapter we'll discuss the various methods of calculating percentage rent.

The concept came into vogue at the same time as large enclosed regional malls. These malls had dozens of tenants that attracted a large geographic market and resulted in considerable consumer traffic. The rents were effectively based on a percentage of the tenant's annual sales with a guaranteed minimum rent (thus the term "minimum rent"). The landlord participated in the upside of generating all that consumer traffic.

Percentage rent is akin to a license fee charged by the landlord as compensation and incentive to maximize tenant sales, because it is directly tied to a tenant's sales performance. The concept is that the landlord will work diligently to continuously improve the desirability of the property so the overall property sales increase. It is incented to do so through percentage rent.

The reality of commercial real estate today is that as the expense of creating the space for lease, from the cost of land to development to construction and leasing resulted in the growth of minimum rent that outpaced both total sales growth and sales gross margin. As a result, the amount of the landlord's total revenue derived from percentage rent has steadily decreased. Counterintuitive to the argument against incenting the landlord to attract more customers and sales potential via percentage rent, gross margin is actually decreasing, so tenants rely on more volume per location to maintain the same dollar of profit.

How to Use Percentage Rent to Gain Leverage

Today, percentage rent can be used in a number of different ways in a lease negotiation. It can be used:

- As originally created to act as a license to access a market,

- As a quid pro quo negotiating chip when a tenant asks for an exclusivity concerning its use in the property,
- As a method to increase the minimum rent during negotiations,
- As a 'what if' capture point to a future event, as discussed later, and
- As a concession in a negotiation.

Percentage rent shouldn't be blindly conceded since it can be used in the negotiation in so many different ways.

Here are some different ways percentage rent has been used.

Example #1

A tenant wanted a substantial construction allowance from the landlord, which the landlord wasn't prepared to provide. However, the allowance was also critical to obtaining the minimum rent the landlord desired as part of a refinancing package. In short the negotiation turned on this point: no significant allowance equals no significant minimum rent. The landlord did have a more modest allowance amount tied to the desired minimum rent objective. To bridge the difference between what the landlord was prepared to offer for an allowance and what the tenant wanted, the

86

landlord offered a credit against the percentage rent first accruing equal to the difference. It solidified the lease transaction.

If the tenant entered into a position to pay percentage rent (see the section on percentage rent math), the landlord wasn't really out any income required for the financing exercise because it wasn't factored into the budget for refinancing. Notice too that since it was offered as a credit, no cashflow issues were encountered by the landlord and the full amount of the credit was contingent on the tenant creating an amount of percentage rent payable at least equal to the total credit.

Example #2

Another tenant required rent relief against the contracted rent due to a short term sales issue. The landlord inserted the percentage rent concept as part of the package to protect its income if sales improved during the relief period. Rent relief is covered in depth in Chapter 13.

Example #3

This tenant wanted to downsize their space needs by abandoning the rear portion of the space as surplus 'retail space' and then rent it back at a much lower storage rent rate. The landlord was agreeable to the concept for a number of reasons and could not simply average down the tenant's rent over the whole of the space because the landlord needed to support the per square foot rent structure. However, to protect the landlord's income, he added a percentage rent clause.

Ultimately, the tenant's sales didn't decreased in the smaller space as much as the tenant believed they would and the aggregate of the reduced minimum rent from the smaller space, the storage rent on the remainder and the amount of percentage rent paid was more than if the tenant had not downsized. Interestingly, the tenant was still happy because the tenant achieved what they wanted by having a smaller unit size.

Percentage Rent Math

In its simplest form, percentage rent is based on the tenant's sales less the minimum rent paid. Worded differently, the tenant pays the greater of the stipulated percentage rent rate applied to the sales or the minimum rent.

There are many variables to the way percentage rent can be calculated. The most common is whether or not percentage rent is calculated annually, or on some shorter period such as quarterly or monthly. And if it is calculated on a shorter period of time than a full year, is it calculated on a cumulative or direct basis. Here is the difference as illustrated in the examples below:

Lets assume in both cases that the minimum rent is $24,000 per annum, or $2,000 per month. Lets also assume that the percentage rent rate is 8% of gross sales.

The point at which $24,000 is equal to 8% of sales is $300,000; or $25,000 per month. This is called the natural breakpoint.

Lets further assume that the tenant has sales of $26,000 in the first month, $20,500 in the second month and $27,500 in the third month.

If the percent rent is calculated monthly on a cumulative basis over a year, the math looks like this:

Mth	Sales $000	Cumulative Sales	8% of sales to date	Base Rent to date	% Rent
1	26	26,000	2,080	2,000	80
2	20.5	46,500	3,720	4,000	-
3	27.5	74,000	5,920	6,000	-

In reality, even the $80.00 would be refunded if this continued for the year.

If the percentage rent was calculated only on the month's sales, the math looks like this:

Month	Sales ($)	8% of sales for the month	Minimum Rent for the month	Percentage rent payable
1	26,000	2,080	2,000	80
2	20,500	1,640	2,000	-
3	27,500	2,200	2,000	200

The total owed by the tenant is $280.00 for the period and the landlord wouldn't have to refund any of the payments.

Of course, which method that is used is determined by the way the lease is worded.

The example above illustrates percentage rent calculated using a natural breakpoint, which is the point when the minimum rent is equal to the percentage rent factor of the gross sales.

However, the breakpoint can be negotiated. Tenants will want it higher and landlords will want it lower.

The percentage rent factor can also be split at different sales levels; or different factors can be assigned to different categories of merchandise carried by the tenant, based on the gross margin of each category.

The table below outlines typical percentage rent factors used in the retail industry.

TYPICAL PERCENTAGE RENTS

Card & gift shop	5.0 to 8.0%
Drugstore	2.5 to 4.0%
Liquor and wine shop	1.5 to 5.0%
Pet shop	5.0 to 8.0%
Restaurant	4.0 to 7.0%
Supermarket	1.0 to 2.0%

Adapted from *Dollars & Cents of Shopping Centers*, Urban Land Institute, Washington, D.C.

There are three very important aspects to percentage rent that make it an essential component to the landlord's leasing toolbox.

The first is that percentage rent has many variables in how it is calculated, as demonstrated above. Therefore, it is a flexible negotiating tool. The landlord's representative can negotiate how it is paid, when it is paid, the percentage factor, the breakpoint(s) and even exclusions to the sales that make up the gross revenue that the percentage rent is based upon.

The second aspect is that percentage rent is not tied to an expense of the landlord. Minimum rent is tied to the debt covenants. Additional rent is tied to operating costs and property taxes. Consequently, there is not much room for the landlord to negotiate either Minimum rent or Additional rent. Effectively, the landlord is always working with a 'floor' when negotiating either Minimum rent or Additional rent and the landlord should never negotiate below those two floors. Conversely, the landlord is free to negotiate percent rent all the way to zero if need be.

All those variables and the fact that percent rent has no underlying cost associated with it means that percent rent can be used to create different negotiating options that can be used at different times and in different ways during the lease discussion. That is why it is one of the most powerful negotiating tools and the landlord should retain it as much as possible.

The third aspect to percentage rent is that it is tied to the tenant's sales. That brings us to the importance of tenant sales reporting.

The Importance of Tenant Gross Revenue Reporting

As percent rent was being discarded, so too was the requirement for tenants to report gross revenue (often referred to as sales). This is a mistake since it removes one of the landlord's key metrics concerning their property.

Sales information is critical to creating the Story to Sell. The Landlord has only three things to sell a tenant:

1. Space,
2. Time, and
3. Access to a specified or unique market.

One way to verify that your property accesses a market better than another location is providing (non-confidential) gross revenue information about the property or merchandise category.

Tenants also use sales information to model their business proforma, so sales information is a further leasing tool.

In chapter 4 we discuss how the property's gross revenue information can be used to support the minimum rent asking price and how this information can be used to consistently achieve rent greater than the surrounding marketplace.

Tenant sales reports can also alert the landlord to tenants in trouble. The gross revenue information can provide an early warning signal to the landlord about the health of their property.

When used properly, detailed gross revenue information can also help in negotiating a CAP Rate that is lower than prevailing conditions, adding value at the time of a property sale or refinancing.

The Landlord should never forego the opportunity to obtain every applicable tenant's gross revenue information on a regular basis – preferably monthly. Landlords should consider clauses related to sales reporting as boilerplate items in the lease.

What Should be Included in Gross Revenue?

In short, it should be all forms of income from the tenant's location in the property. This includes sales as well as all other forms of revenue the tenant derives. Not all of a tenant's income is from 'sales'. The tenant may also obtain slotting or preferred placement fees from distributors, advertising commissions, handling fees, concessions, licenses, etc.

A lawyer knowledgeable in commercials leases will note appropriate deductions to Gross Revenue, such as returned merchandise, inter-store inventory exchanges, a sale of the business or the sale of store fixtures no longer used, taxes on sales, etc.

There are also certain tenants who cannot report gross revenue information, or where the information is not meaningful to the landlord's objectives. The most common are government agency tenants, banks, non-profit tenants, etc.

Expect that a savvy tenant will push back on a broad interpretation of gross revenue, particularly if the reporting of gross revenue is tied to an obligation for percent rent.

However, the rebuttal is that all that gross revenue is obtained from the premises because the tenant has access to a unique market; that in turn, allows the tenant to charge those fees. It is the landlord's license to that market, if you will (relative to the impact on percent rent); or is an accurate reflection of the value of that market (relative to reporting without percent rent) that the landlord needs to know and understand to maximize future sales potential through merchandising.

The confluence between internet sales and retail locations (known as clicks to bricks) also needs to be addressed in the definition of Gross Revenue in the lease.

A growing number of retail sales occur online with in-store delivery, or occur online as a result of the familiarity the consumer has with the brand through its physical location in the landlord's property. There are also retail showrooms, where the product is simply displayed and all orders are taken online.

The Landlord should ensure that the definition Gross Revenue captures these events. We believe the wording we use for our clients accomplishes this. If you would like to learn more about this or any of the services we provide please email pdmorris@greensteadcg.com

At the very least, being aware of and discussing the various forms of income the tenant receives or expects to receive as a result of a location in the landlord's property gives the landlord arguments and proof to support the business terms of the transaction.

IN SUMMARY

Percentage rent is one of the most powerful negotiating tools a landlord has in their leasing toolbox.

Percentage rent is flexible and has variables in how it is constructed, reported and used during the term of the lease.

Gross Revenue reporting is a key metric that every landlord should retain in almost every lease because the information provides critical leasing and operational data.

Gross revenue is more than just the sales from the location.

Chapter 6
Structuring Additional Rent

**'There is a reason it is one of the most
negotiated portions of the lease.'**

Almost all leases define Additional Rent as
all remittances to the Landlord with the
exception of Minimum Rent and Percentage
Rent. The landlord should look at the make
up of the Additional Rent charged to
maximize their negotiating position and cash
flow. This is more than just minimizing
recoverable charges to gain more Minimum
Rent. How the Additional Rent is structured
plays a key role as well.

The most common practice in retail leases is
the concept of Triple Net leases. Triple Net is
a term that has been used for decades to
describe the landlord's recovery of
maintenance, insurance and tax expenses in

addition to the Minimum Rent. In contrast, Gross Rent is one sum that includes every cost of the landlord and the Minimum Rent.

However, in recent years some landlords are moving away from Triple Net and instead charge a service fee. We'll discuss that concept later in this chapter.

Some of the most negotiated clauses in the lease pertain to which expenses should be included as part of what the tenant pays in the minimum rent and which should be deemed recoverable charges in addition to minimum rent.

In the majority of leases, the recoverable costs are lumped into two categories: Operating Expenses and Realty Taxes. Operating Costs can also be divided into Common Area Maintenance (also known as CAM) and utilities.

Many leases have a formula to determine the tenant's share of the total costs of these items, typically calculated on a proportionate basis using the area of the tenant's premises divided by the total gross leasable area of the shopping centre. That fraction is sometimes converted into a specified percentage of the costs and stated in the lease; or the fraction is applied to the total costs.

It is a common practice to quote lease rates by lumping all the operating costs and taxes into either the two separate numbers (ie: operating costs are $X and taxes are $Y) or one number (representing CAM and Taxes combined).

In this chapter we will challenge how these costs are structured in the lease and presented in lease negotiations. The current system used by many landlords is flawed in the way it is drafted in the lease and thought of in the management of the property. As such, it costs landlords in slippage of recoverable expenses, a loss of maximizing the total rent package during negotiation, increased management costs and damage to landlord/tenant relationships.

Earlier it was noted that the lease should not be a universal template from "off the shelf" but should be tailored to each project and each landlord's operating philosophy. We'll expand on that concept in this chapter.

Recoverable costs shouldn't be lumped into one or two pools and the method of apportioning the costs should be different depending on the expense.

On the surface this may seem as though it should increase management's time and cost as compared to the 'one pot' approach.

*"**Doing the job right the first time is always cheaper**" Phillip Crosby, Quality Management Consultant*

Issues arise when tenants want to understand the make-up of recoverable expenses. It is always more time intensive to forensically mine accounting data than to segregate it at the start.

How should they be pooled?

Common Area Maintenance (CAM): The only items to go into CAM should be expenses related to the common areas. There should be no costs relating to any premises in this pool of expenses.

Tenant Services: These are expenses related to services provided to leased premises en masse, grouped to a portion of the tenants or individually.

Realty Taxes: Due to the cost of realty taxes as a percentage of the total costs and the way they can be assessed, billed and applied, the realty taxes require their own pool.

Lets examine each pool in greater detail.

Common Area Maintenance (CAM)

CAM costs include the cost of maintaining, operating and managing the common areas of the property. These should be described better as operating costs that include maintenance, amongst other things. Operating costs include but aren't limited to the following:

(1) the cost of all insurance obtained by the Landlord for the Shopping Centre, including insurance for loss of Rent and for the amount of losses incurred (including losses in respect of unsettled claims) or claims paid below insurance deductible amounts;

(2) the cost of cleaning the Common Areas, including snow removal where applicable, sweeping, refuse storage and removal and similar expenses;

(3) Common Areas maintenance, repair, replacement and supervision, including the costs of policing and security, gardening, landscaping, cleaning and decorating;

(4)   parking lot maintenance and repair, including, but not limited to parking lot striping, cleaning and signage;

(5)   auditing, accounting, legal and other professional or consulting fees and disbursements incurred and the cost of personnel reasonably attributable to the administration, operation, management, repair, security and supervision of the Shopping Centre or otherwise employed by the Landlord or a management company in connection with the management, maintenance and operation of the Shopping Centre;

(6)   the cost of Common Areas lighting, including parking areas, utilities and repair and maintenance of lamp standards and related facilities and the cost of purchase, rental and maintenance of any Common Area canopies, furniture and facilities;

(7)   the total annual amortization of major capital costs, major repairs and major replacements;

(8)   Shopping Centre signage;

(9)   the cost of the supplies, material and labour used by the Landlord in the operation and maintenance of the Common Areas and the Shopping Centre;

(10) depreciation and reasonable carrying costs on the undepreciated capital cost of heating, ventilating and air-conditioning equipment and machinery, equipment and fixtures which by their nature require periodic or substantial replacement;

(11) the cost of all service contracts, including without limitation, mechanical, electrical, security, cleaning or elevator maintenance;

(12) business taxes, property taxes not otherwise included as a cost to the Tenant;

(13) heating, ventilating and air-conditioning costs related to the common areas only – not tenant premises – as you will see why;

(14) the cost for fuel or other energy for heating, ventilating and air-conditioning systems, and for electricity, steam, water, oil, gas or other power required in connection with the use and operation of the Shopping Centre, including lighting, but excluding the Tenant's exclusive heating, ventilation and air-conditioning costs;

(15) rental of equipment, sanitary control, purchase of stationery supplies and other materials in regard to the management of the Shopping Centre, fire alarm systems and the monitoring and maintenance of same;

(16) all rents, expenses, fees, charges and other amounts which are the responsibility of the Landlord under the Shopping Centre Head Lease and/or any sublease of any premises forming part of the Shopping Centre, or which are incurred by the Landlord pursuant to the Shopping Centre Head Lease (if the landlord is

a head lessee pursuant to a ground lease);

(17) the cost of all licenses and permits and any inspection fees incurred by the Landlord in respect of the Common Areas and the Shopping Centre;

(18) the cost of operating and maintaining management offices, security offices, utility rooms, meter rooms, maintenance and storage areas, janitorial and custodial rooms and facilities for the storage of equipment serving the Common Areas, including the fair market rent for such areas;

(19) technology expenses, including expenses incurred to establish a website related to the Shopping Centre and/or to advertise the Shopping Centre on the internet;

(20) any financial contributions required to be made by the Landlord pursuant to any easements or use/cost-sharing agreements with other strata corporations, owners or occupants of

adjacent or neighbouring buildings, lands or air space parcels to which the Landlord is bound from time to time; and

(21) such other operating costs, charges and expenditures of any nature as may be incurred by the Landlord in respect of the proper preservation, protection, maintenance, and operation of the Common Areas.

Fairly exhaustive list, isn't it? In fact, the list is too long for the tenants to spend time managing these functions in addition to their own business so either the landlord or the property manager manages the operation, maintenance and repair of the common facilities on behalf of all the tenants.

The concept of the tenants sharing in the cost of operating the areas they have access to in common is actually born in the single net tenant lease.

In a single net tenant lease, the tenant pays the landlord a minimum rent to occupy the building and/or land. In addition, the tenant pays either to its own account or to the landlord, all costs associated with the land so the landlord bears no additional expense.

108

In a multiple tenant building those costs are shared, but not necessarily equally. And that is an important point.

Anchor tenants often do not pay a proportionate share of the operating costs for a variety of reasons. Therefore, to keep the landlord whole, the share calculation should exclude the anchor's area from the denominator and the anchor's contribution to the operating costs should be deducted from the total before the apportionment. Likewise, if the property contains both interior common areas and exterior tenants, expect the exterior tenants to not want to pay a portion of the expenses relating to the interior common areas. Again both the exterior tenant contributions and their respective area(s) should be deducted. The lease wording must capture these concepts.

The concept of sharing common operating costs becomes much more complicated in a mixed-use development as you will see in that chapter.

Let's revisit how the lease is structured in a single tenant asset for a moment and apply the same thought process to a multi-tenant property, either for a single use (such as retail) or in a mixed-use property.

The minimum rent paid by the tenant in a single tenant property covers the use of the space, but not all the maintenance, operation and taxes of the building or grounds. The tenant either pays for that themselves or reimburses the landlord for those expenses. The concept is similar in a multi-tenant property, but rather than having the tenants themselves work out how to manage those costs and have the work done, they contract with the landlord to manage the common areas as part of the lease.

The costs of the daily management and operation are included in recoverable operating expenses (item #5) because it is a service provided to the tenants so they don't have to do the work themselves. In turn, the landlord has either in-house property managers and facility operators conduct the work, or they contract this to other firms that specialize in third party management. This begs the question of who is overseeing the management of the common area?

Management Fee V. Administration Fee

The management fee charged by a third party manager, or in-house staff, covers the cost of the daily management of the common area. However, the landlord must still oversee the management per the contract implied in the lease. Therefore, the landlord should be compensated for this oversight.

In a large property this is usually added to the total operating costs and taxes. The number fluctuates between 10% to 15%, with 15% being the most common. To ensure there isn't confusion between the daily management fee and the costs of oversight, this reimbursement of the landlord's time in the oversight of the management should be called the "administration fee."

In a small property, such as a grocery anchored retail plaza, the operating expenses are comparatively lower than in the large mall. However, the landlord's time is still a fixed cost. To recognize this, the landlord of a small property should charge an administration fee of 5% on the total rent (Minimum rent, Additional Rent and Percentage Rent) rather than 15% on the operating costs and taxes alone.

A tenant may argue that the 'standard' for management fees are 3% or a similarly lower number. The landlord should counter noting that the management fee is in item 5 and the administration fee is for the landlord's oversight of the management. The landlord can also continue noting the extrapolation of the premise of a single tenant lease.

If the difference becomes a sticking point in the negotiation, we advise clients to calculate the difference on an annual per square foot basis and discount the minimum rent rather than reduce the percentage. Why?

There are three main reasons. The first is psychological and the other two are financial.

1. The landlord should always retain the position that is must be compensated outside of the minimum rent for services it provides to the common area. Remember that we said earlier that some of the most negotiated clauses in the lease pertain to which expenses should be included as part of what the tenant pays in the minimum rent and which should be deemed recoverable charges in addition to minimum rent. This is consistent with keeping the two separate.

2. The dollar value of the percentage will increase over the term of the lease as costs increase, whereas the minimum rent deduction is fixed in time at the beginning of the lease. This mitigates the actual dollar amount the landlord foregoes over time. For example, lets assume that the minimum rent deduction equal to a 1% reduction of a

(5%) administration fee is 20 cents per square foot per annum. Instead of reducing the administration fee from 5% to 4%, the landlord reduces the minimum rent by 20 cents per square foot per annum.

If the total amount of the rent the administration fee is charged against rises by just $4.01 per square foot per annum over the term, then the landlord is further ahead by retaining the 5% with a 20-cent base rent reduction than reducing the administration fee by 1%.

3. Unless the percentage rent has a fixed breakpoint, the natural point at which the tenant starts paying percentage rent is reduced because of the deduction to the minimum rent. While not significant relative to cashflow, it is important when calculating value.

Back to operating costs and how those are recovered in the lease.

Many landlords convert the proportionate share fraction into a specified percentage of the costs payable by each tenant. This assumes that the nature of the property will remain static over the term of the lease, unless additional wording is used to allow for adjustments to the percentage.

It is also important to note that the most common definition for the denominator is the gross <u>leasable</u> area of the property. This includes all areas intended for lease, whether or not they are leased. Some landlords do change the definition to gross <u>leased</u> area, which reduces the denominator by any vacancy. This is very uncommon and unpopular with tenants.

Most tenants insist on gross leasable area arguing that the costs for the landlord's inability to lease space shouldn't be borne by the existing tenants. The result of any vacancy is a shortfall on operating cost recoveries that is then borne by the landlord, often called "recovery, or vacancy, slippage". There is a way to mitigate the shortfall that we will discuss shortly.

There are also two other important concepts relating to the common operating costs that every landlord should practice, but seem to be missed in many leases.

In item #7 of the list of operating costs, amortization of major expenses is noted.

Major expenses are incurred up front by the landlord but the amortization of the expense is allocated annually. Since the landlord is effectively loaning the tenants the funds to complete the work, the landlord should also obtain interest on amortization just as the landlord would on any other loan. The lease should specifically include language that provides for this and should state the amount of interest to be charged.

Item #18 includes all the costs of operating and maintaining a variety of service areas including an imputed rent on those areas. This harkens back to the inclusiveness of the recoveries from a single tenant property. That a meter room serving the common area, for example, isn't inside and included in a tenant's specific space doesn't negate the rental value of the room. Many times this compensation to the landlord is overlooked.

There are deductions to the operating costs. The common deductions pertain to the landlord's costs to obtain minimum rent, such a structural repairs, mortgage payments, leasing commissions and alike.

Caps, Base Years and Limitations

If we agree the concept of operating cost recoveries in a net lease is that the tenants pay for all the costs of operating and maintaining the common facilities; then caps, or other limitations on a tenant's contribution toward those costs should be avoided.

Conversely, tenants want the comfort in knowing that the landlord will manage the common area responsibly. Therefore, some tenants ask the landlord to limit the operating costs and to limit an increase in those costs in each subsequent year of the term. Typically, the tenant will agree to an increase equal to the rate of inflation (also called the "Consumer Price Index" or "CPI").

There are a number of problems with this concept and its derivatives.

Remember that the lease is not for a specific point in time, but spans several years. A cap and escalator clause that is encompassing of all the operating costs noted above can create a recovery shortfall resulting from those expense items that the landlord has absolutely no control over. These include insurance costs, snow removal costs (in regions prone to snow), realty taxes, and utilities. Additionally, depending on the age of the building and the term of the lease, amortized expenses should also be excluded from the cap.

If a cap and escalator is required to complete the transaction, it is important to exclude these items from the cap.

Savvy tenants will also attempt to negotiate a cap equal to the lesser of the previous year's actual expenses plus the escalator or the previous year's prepayment amount plus the escalator. This clause is particularly problematic in new properties, where the landlord has made a best estimate of the operating costs. If that estimate is incorrect, there could be a perpetual recovery shortfall during the term.

The best way to protect the landlord's ability to gain a full recovery of operating expenses is to consider the operating expense clauses as non-negotiable.

This is much easier to do when the additional rent pools separate the costs of operating the common areas from providing services to premises.

The Emerging Trend of the Service Charge

Before discussing services to the premises however, there is a trend to a common area service charge concept, which is actually a throwback to the time when retail leases were all encompassing 'gross' leases.

Effectively, this is the same as placing a cap on the CAM charges. The concept is much easier to administer to if the expenses related to specific premises are not included in the common area operating charges as outlined later.

The service charge captures all types of controllable expenses in one number that is charged to the tenants. This amount escalates annually either by the rate of inflation or a 'greater of' a fixed percentage rate, such as 3.5% per annum, or the rate of inflation.

The advantage to both the landlord and the tenant is that a service charge reduces the cost of administration and removes a lot of the negotiation. Effectively, the landlord says to the tenant that this is a number and in that number we will manage the common area. There is no need to negotiate all the 21 points of what makes up the operating costs.

Some tenants are leery of the concept because they think the landlord also includes a profit margin in the sum. And rightly so, since some landlords do add a profit margin. In fact, our clients are advised to add a small contingency into the service charge. However, the landlord needs to be aware of the occupancy charges of other properties and with the total rent a tenant can afford relative to the sales. This comparison can be used in addressing the tenant's concern about potential profit in the service charge number during the negotiation.

The caveat to determining the service charge is to remove from the charge figure those costs which are beyond the landlords control. These include insurance costs, snow removal costs (in regions prone to snow), realty taxes, utilities and amortized expenses.

The potential downsides to a flat-rate operating cost service charge are unforeseen events that either dramatically increase one or more previously controllable costs, or decrease the property gross leasable area upon which the service charge is based.

The latter of the two events is more likely to occur and can happen simply by remerchandising such combining a number of smaller spaces into a new anchor or sub-anchor and allowing that tenant to have a service charge or other contribution that is less than previously realized.

For the same reason, we advise landlord's not to convert the numerator/denominator concept for determining the tenant's portion of triple net charges into a percentage. The landlord could face a recovery shortfall if the denominator changes for any reason.

To protect the landlord's interests the cost of operating the common areas should be considered non-negotiable, whether the landlord uses a triple net or service charge concept.

Tenant Services

Landlords often lump services provided to tenants and premises into common area operating costs. This is a mistake for a few reasons:

- it convolutes the concept of common area operating costs being only for expenses related to areas in common. That overlapping of what should be in CAM causes tenants to be concerned about other costs that aren't truly in the common interest and makes them more vigilant in their negotiations.
- it exposes the landlord to recovery shortfalls due to vacancy or anchor contribution shortfalls.

-   it inflates the true cost of operating the centre while reducing the tenant's true operating costs for their premises.

What are Tenant Services expenses? These include all the expenses that are incurred by the landlord on behalf of the tenant's operation in the premises. These include: premise utilities, waste removal (of waste generated in the premises as compared to waste in the common area), additional utilities resulting from the tenant being open longer than the balance of the property, additional or supplemental security, storefront cleaning and – the big one – heating, ventilation and air conditioning (HVAC) maintenance, repairs and replacement related to the tenant's premises.

Tenant Services expenses can be apportioned on a different basis than Operating Costs so there is no shortfall to the landlord in providing these services. These expenses are easily understood and accepted by the tenant as costs directly related to the operation of their business.

In addition, since most of these are operational expenses rather than premise costs, the tenant may, and the landlord should, remove them from calculations for rent to sales ratios (also known as Gross Rent Occupancy Costs, or GROC for short).

While they should always be disclosed to prospective tenants, having Tenant Services listed separately and apart from CAM, or Operating expenses, favorably positions the property's asking rates against those landlords who lump all the costs under the one umbrella.

The third pool is realty taxes.

Realty Taxes

Realty taxes can be apportioned on the basis of a per square foot share of the total taxes or based on the assessed value of each rent value, since most assessments are completed using the income approach to valuation.

In the first method to the calculation, the total bill is divided by the area and then multiplied by the area of each premises. Therefore, the tenants are each contributing an equal per square foot amount to the overall realty tax.

In the second method, each tenant's rent is factored as a disproportionate contribution to the overall tax bill. While this produces a more accurate allocation of each tenant's respective realty tax burden, it is cumbersome to administer to and is not universally accepted.

What is more important to the landlord however, is to retain the ability to switch to different methods of allocating tax should the need arise; to allow for some tenants to be allocated using the second method if their tax contribution would be disproportionately low using the first method; and the timing of the payments by the tenants as compared to the timing of the expense.

The landlord should not use the same proportionate share methodology used for Operating or CAM costs concerning the allocation realty taxes because of the various ways taxes can be allocated and collected.

The landlord also needs to be aware of the cash flow implications of how the recovery is structured. Realty taxes are typically paid once a year or on an accelerated schedule such as a period of 3 – 6 months. Given the landlord's cash reserves, the landlord may opt to bill the tenants of the property once, at the time of the tax bill, for the full amount; collect taxes in advance on an accelerated basis or on a $1/12^{th}$ basis over the course of the year. Whatever method is used, it needs to be clearly stated in the lease and discussed during the negotiations.

There is one other, often overlooked, aspect to the allocation of realty taxes. Since realty taxes are based on the income approach to value, the value that the tax rate is billed on naturally excludes vacant space. By extension, it is logical to reduce the total area in the denominator by the vacancy factor used in the valuation, in addition to the other adjustments previously noted. This way, the tenants and not the landlord are paying their portion of taxes. However, expect sophisticated tenants to push back on this concept simply because it is not widely used and included in the definition of the area for tax recovery in most leases.

Our customizable lease form provides for the landlord to adjust the method of billing of taxes by tenant and in each year.

IN SUMMARY

Operating costs (also commonly referred to as CAM) should only include costs related to the common areas of the property.

Tenant Services should be a separate pool of expenses and these relate to services provided to premises.

Realty Taxes should not be lumped into CAM and should be treated as a separate cost pool.

An annually escalating Operating Cost Service Charge is an emerging trend and should be treated in the same way as CAM caps are negotiated with and exclusion of those items out of the control of the landlord.

Chapter 7
Negotiating Renewal Options

'Its time to stop lease renewal and extensions.'

An option to renew the Lease falls under the broad category of Tenant Benefit Clauses because it is a clause requested by the Tenant that only benefits the Tenant. It is an option that, unless otherwise stated, is exclusively under their control.

As noted previously, all clauses that diminish the landlords' control of their investment should be avoided; or, at the very least mitigated.

Here is a major concern about an option to renew the lease that seems to be lost on many landlords as it appears in almost every lease where the option has been granted. An option to renew the lease is just that. It is an opportunity for the tenant to renew the legal contract it negotiated for a further term.

Most times, options are provided in the initial lease negotiated between the landlord and the tenant. Consider the relative negotiating strength of that first lease. The landlord is typically 'selling' the tenant on the property and the knowledgeable tenant is unsure of their performance and will want to mitigate its risk. As a result, there are perhaps more concessions given by the landlord, than when the property has proven itself to the tenant.

If it is a good location, the tenant will want to lock in those concessions. If it is a mediocre to poor location, the tenant will simply not exercise its option in order to further negotiate the lease with the landlord or relocate.

Another issue with renewing the lease document, is that things change over the term of the lease, despite the lease negotiators' best attempts to make the lease as flexible as possible. Laws can change that affect the operations of the property, zoning can change, tenant merchandising practices evolve and technologies are invented. Notice too that all these examples are beyond the direct control of the landlord.

There are still leases in effect today that date back before the days of personal computers, let alone the internet. There are leases that predate grocery stores providing prepared meals, drugs or clothing.

The landlord now has leases that may cause leasing, operating and financial concerns due to these types of changes.

Landlords also want to position their asset favorably in the event of a sale. Many landlords like to use their own lease form after purchasing a property. By limiting the current lease to the initial term vs. the term and all the options means a purchaser can 'convert' the tenant to their lease form sooner. While probably a minor consideration, it is still one to note.

Many tenants simply ask for the renewal option because they want to secure their tenancy in the property. They don't want to be in a lease that is 5 to 10 years long, build the business and find they no longer have their location to enjoy their hard work or to reap the rewards and sell the business.

To limit renewal options, the landlord should establish a guide concerning which types of tenants are granted the option and which are not. As a rule of thumb, single store specialty stores should not be granted options; or, if required, at most a single option provided.

Restaurants typically require a series of options due to the capital intensive nature of their business; national chains and anchor tenants will always demand a number of options.

Renewal of Lease, or.......

Since options only work in the tenant's favour, the question needs to be asked about an alternative that is more in the landlord's favor. Or at least is more on balance in protecting the landlord risks.

The answer comes in two parts. It depends on what is being renewed and how it is structured.

In many cases, the tenant is simply asking for security of the space. Therefore, the landlord should offer a renewal of the <u>tenancy</u>, not a renewal of the lease. The renewal of tenancy lets the tenant know they can secure the space, but the underlying lease document is not being renewed and a new document must be negotiated near the end of the term.

This allows the landlord to accomplish two things: the landlord can update the lease if needed, and the landlord can assess their relative negotiating strength and claw-back earlier concessions.

The renewal of tenancy clause we advise our clients to use states that the tenant will sign the landlord's then standard lease. We use this wording specifically. On the face of it, all lease wording negotiation is removed at the renewal and the tenant must sign the standard lease as presented. In practice, we use this to retain negotiating leverage and, depending on the negotiations, provide some concessions and/or trade concessions for higher rent.

If there must be a renewal in the document, a renewal of tenancy is always more in the Landlord's favor than a renewal of the actual lease.

The renewal must also be structured in such a way that the landlord doesn't end up in a worse position than it was in prior to the renewal. While this may seem obvious, it occurs time and again because the landlord doesn't do two key things during the initial lease negotiation.

The first item is to place conditions on the tenant's ability to exercise the renewal other than to simply provide notice.

Some key conditions include:

- The tenant must be the tenant originally named in the lease, or (if need be) an approved assignee. The option to renew was granted to the original tenant at the time of the initial negotiation. It may have come up because that specific tenant was a desirable tenant and had the negotiating power.

  We advise our clients to not include the 'approved assignee' wording if possible. Please read the chapter on assignments to understand why.

- The tenant must be in full and continuous occupation of the premises and be conducting business on a daily basis. This is one of those items that can easily catch the landlord off guard if they don't cross check their concessions and clauses.

  If the tenant has the ability to cease operating from the premises but continue to control the premises under the lease, the landlord certainly doesn't want to allow that tenant to be able to exercise a renewal. This is particularly true if the tenant also enjoys a restrictive covenant in the lease. Please read the chapter on exclusivities and restrictive covenants.

- The tenant must not have been in default or breach of the lease. We advise clients that this should be worded as broadly as possible even though many tenants will push back and ask that the wording be modified so that the tenant can't be in default at the time of renewal. That doesn't resolve the basic problem of a tenant that doesn't abide by the lease. A poor tenant could cure the breach once, exercise the renewal and then fall back to their old ways.

- The renewal clause should have some form of performance criteria before the tenant is allowed to renew the lease. The landlord should only grant renewal options to tenants that benefit the business objectives of the landlord and the well being of the centre. The performance clause could be a formula tied to the tenant's sales and the sales of the shopping centre, a minimum gross revenue threshold, or the payment of percent rent.

- Likewise, the renewal may also be tied to a refurbishment of the premises depending on the initial term and the extent of the original leasehold improvements.

Setting Minimum Rent on Renewal

The second thing that must be done during the initial lease is outline how the minimum rent for the renewal period will be determined. Establishing the amount of minimum rent payable during the renewal term is sometimes more difficult than agreeing to the minimum rent for the initial term. On one hand the tenant wants rent that is either below or at the rent they would have to pay at the time of the renewal. On the other hand, the landlord wants minimum rent that is at least the same rent they would obtain from another party at the time of the renewal, and preferably higher.

The obvious issue is that neither party has an accurate crystal ball as to what rents will be in 5 or more years in the future.

To mitigate the rent risk tenants ask for either a pre-negotiated rent amount they feel comfortable with; or 'fair market rent'. In the latter case, the tenant will want to have a third party, such as an arbitrator or mediator, determine what 'fair market rent' is to be if the two sides can't agree. Some tenants will negotiate hard for the lesser of the pre-negotiated rent or the fair market rent.

None of these options are good for the landlord as they are typically written. Remember that the renewal option itself is only beneficial to the tenant, so these types of rent structures only compound the issue for the landlord.

The detriments of pre-negotiated rents and 'lesser of' formulas are self explanatory. But how can a fair market rent be detrimental to the landlord? Most people would argue that the landlord should achieve what the general market bears and therefore the landlord will be in no worse position. Indeed most leases are written with 'fair market rent' clauses that capture the general rent in the marketplace.

However, if the landlord has created a Story to Sell, as suggested in this book, and has taken steps to lay claim to a unique market that only that property can access, then general market rent should not apply.

Why is this important?

The landlord can only control their own property. A nearly identical property - and space - in terms of size, configuration, community, etc. may have widely different rent than the landlord has for their property. The rent at the other property may be negatively influenced by any number of things including: high recoverable expenses, owner's lack of market knowledge, a desire by the owner to provide some form of loss leader, etc.

Therefore, the landlord negotiating the renewal is attempting to manage and control *their* asset based on the actions (and agendas) of *other* landlords who do not have an interest in this property. Additionally, the tenant is comparing the rent of other properties that aren't the property under negotiation.

This is not a sustainable business model, yet it is perpetuated in lease after lease.

Of course, the other property may also have higher rent but the tenant will immediately discount that property and seek other properties with rents that are less than our landlord is seeking in order to support the tenant's negotiating position.

Obviously, the tenant has the stronger negotiating position when using fair market rent.

To retain the landlord's position and to accurately reflect that the rent for the renewal period is for the property the tenant actually occupies, the landlord can agree that the rent would be the same rent the landlord would otherwise obtain for that space or a comparable space in that specific property. That is the fair rent for <u>that</u> space.

Other Considerations

It may sometimes become necessary to renew the lease document rather than the tenancy. In those cases, it is important for the landlord, their asset manager, property manager, lease negotiator, etc. to review the original lease and insert wording in the lease extension document that removes landlord obligations that only occurred for the initial lease such as leasing incentives, construction allowances, free rent, etc. as well as noting what new obligations the tenant may have, such as a refurbishment of the premises, if part of the renewal provisions.

Whether renewing or extending the lease document or the tenancy it is also important to note that the number of remaining options are reduced by one. If there was only one option, then it should be specifically noted in the document that there are no further renewal options.

In Summary

Lease renewal or extension options only favor the Tenant.

What is being renewed and the structure of the clause play a vital role in retaining the landlord's negotiating position. It is always preferable to the landlord's position to renew the tenancy, not the lease.

The ability to exercise an option to renew should always be conditioned by a number of factors.

Fair Market Rent as it is typically understood and drafted into leases is not fair to the landlord.

138

Chapter 8
Structuring a Use Clause

A well conceived use clause is vital to proper merchandising , sales and rent maximization and tenant harmony.

In reading hundreds of leases it seems that the clause that outlines the permitted use of the premises mostly does not get the attention it deserves in the lease negotiation.

An effective retail property relies on three attributes: merchandising, massing and market. Forget the adage of "Location, Location, Location."

In order to create the Story to Sell the Landlord relies on these three attributes and each tenant's use clause plays a significant role in designing the merchandising of the property.

Here is an actual, poorly written use clause from a lease:

"...the Premises will be solely for the purpose of a licensed sit-down restaurant and for take out and delivery and a lounge. The cuisine will be primarily Middle Eastern, Western and European."

There are many business issues with this clause including a lack of clarity around what constitutes any of the listed cuisine types.

A good use clause on the other hand should be detailed and yet broad enough to permit the tenant merchandising scope within their business concept.

An excellent way to do this is to create a hierarchy of the primary use, a secondary or ancillary use(s) and, in some situations, common products. In each case, it is always best to list the products, merchandise or services sold rather than the general concept. For example, the wording should be something along the lines of:

" the primary use is the sale at retail of [followed by a list of products or services that will make up the bulk of the business], and as ancillary to such primary use the sale at retail of [another list of complimentary product lines]."

Since retail concepts evolve and change it is always better to focus on the types of products and services rather than defaulting to a generic term for a concept. A prime example –though there are many – is "women's wear". There are casual, athletic, petite, larger size, fast fashion, designer, maternity, bridal, uniform, mature, yoga and other types of specialty retailers under the broad definition of women's wear.

To properly merchandise the property and to avoid internal competition from tenants cannibalizing other tenant's sales, it is important to distinguish between the various types of "women's wear" in the merchandising plan.

A properly constructed use clause that has each tenant's product mix well defined also avoids the internal competition that occurs when the property has several similar categories of merchants. Not only does this aid in good tenant relations, because tenant A can't accuse the Landlord of duplicating their use and killing their business by leasing to tenant B; but it should prompt market expansion since the two tenants aren't after the identical customer.

This is an important point when considering the merchandising mix of the property and is part of the second attribute of massing.

Consider the potential success of a property that is focused on women's wear and the different merchants reflect each of the individual segments noted above from casual wear to yoga apparel as compared to a property where each of the tenants have overlapping products as they chase customers.

If the property has multiple on-premise consumption food tenants in close proximity, such as a food court or restaurant area, it is even more important to segregate the product offering of each tenant to provide the customer with a breadth of choice and to avoid product infighting between operators.

One way to handle this is to add a third category to the use clause to handle all the items they all have in common such a beverages. Here is an example of how this works. We will assume that the food court has a burger operation, a fish and chip operation, a sandwich shop and a Mexican restaurant.

If we were to chart the uses, it might look like the following chart, in very broad terms:

Tenant	Primary Use	Ancillary Use	Common Use
Burger	Hamburgers Chicken-Burgers	Fish Burgers, Veggie-Burgers and French Fries	Pop, Water, Coffee, Tea, etc.
Fish & Chips	Deep Fried Fish, Grilled Fish, Fries served with these items	French Fries (sold individually), Fish Burgers and Fish Sandwiches	Pop, Water, Coffee, Tea, etc.
Sandwich	A variety of sandwiches (all named)	Fish Sandwiches, Salads (named), Soup	Pop, Water, Coffee, Tea, etc.
Mexican	A variety of Mexican entrees (all named)	Taco Salad, Tortilla Soup	Pop, Water, Coffee, Tea, etc.

Notice how the primary use – the product that accounts for the majority of sales – for the burger operation excludes fish burgers but the fish burger is listed as an ancillary item. Likewise the fish and chip shop also has the fish burger as an ancillary item.

All the tenants recognize that the items listed in the common use will be universally sold.

While all this may seem like additional negotiating work with little real benefit, it eases the management time in managing the merchandise mix, provides clarity around the leasing function and merchandise mix, and is most helpful if the landlord must provide an exclusivity covenant.

Restrictive Or Exclusive Use Covenant

A restrictive use or exclusive use covenant is another example of a Tenant Benefit Clause™ (also known as a "TBC") that only benefits the tenant. Effectively, the covenant works to limit competition in the property.

It bears repeating that any tenant benefit clauses should be avoided at all costs; however, sometimes an exclusive use clause is needed to close the deal.

Regional and national tenants will push hard for as many tenant benefit clauses as possible, particularly those that affect their sales performance. Remember that after the basic financial terms have been agreed to the balance of the negotiation is risk mitigation. Having the sole right to sell something in the property is a sales risk mitigation tool used by the tenant.

If a prospective tenant ask for an exclusivity clause, the landlord should investigate the reason for the request further. Even though may be very apparent why the tenant is asking – to protect their sales potential, the answer the tenant gives provides a powerful negotiating platform for the landlord. It sets up the negotiation to give the landlord options for a "positive No" response. Here are a few:

The first option depends on the amount of vacancy in the property and the tenant's proposed use. If the property is almost full and the use is unique to the property the landlord can simply state that it isn't needed given the occupancy and the tenant's unique use. The landlord can point out that with the limited vacancy remaining, it is the landlord's preference to lease the remaining space to other uses.

Another option is to introduce percent rent as a quid pro quo, if it isn't already on the table. Alternatively, the landlord can introduce a different percent rate or break point if percent rent has already been agreed to. The reason percent rent is so effective is that both the restrictive and percent rent are tied to overall sales performance. Therefore, it is easy to point out the correlation.

Along the same lines, the landlord can counter with an adjustment in the minimum rent in exchange for the exclusivity clause since the clause adds value to the lease. This takes some more negotiating as the tenant may not perceive the interconnection between the two.

In introducing either a percent rent clause or adjustment or a change in the minimum rent, the tenant now has an either/or decision. When used in combination with first option, the tenant may believe the added cost is not worth having the restrictive clause.

If the prospective tenant adamant that they need the clause to protect sales, then the landlord should determine if the tenant is mostly concerned about the start-up sales. This allows the landlord the ability to limit the exclusive to a certain period of time, if the landlord must provide the clause. This can range from one year to the initial term of the lease, but not any renewals.

If the landlord is placed in the position where they must entertain an exclusivity, then the following is important, but often overlooked.

The restrictive covenant should be limited to the following two items only:

1. It should be limited only to the act of the landlord leasing another space in the property to a competing use. Leasing is the landlord's business, nothing more in this case. Many use clauses erroneously refer to the landlord not permitting any other tenant to use, occupy, stock, or sell or carry on business as "X,Y,Z." The "X,Y,Z" is typically worded as a general concept, which we have already agreed is a bad idea in a use clause. It is worse in an exclusive covenant. Aside from being a level of care that the landlord is not compensated for, this type of wording carries additional risks because of the broad wording in relation to the evolving nature of retail over the prospective term.

2. It should be limited only to the primary use of the tenant. This drives the restriction to products and not concepts. It also protects the landlord's ability to introduce other merchants that don't directly compete, but may have some overlapping

merchandise or services as ancillary uses.

Any agreement on a restrictive should exclude all anchor tenants, since they generally have very broad use clauses due to their size and nature of business.

Any existing tenants in the property should be excluded too, since it would be a monumental and expensive task to have an existing tenant unwind their merchandising. Likewise, all of the existing tenants' heirs, assigns, successors and replacements should also be excluded so the current merchandising can be retained. Your lawyer will have appropriate wording.

Recall the poorly worded use clause example? This tenant also had a poorly worded restrictive covenant. Here is what it said:

"....the Landlord shall not lease any other premises in the Shopping Centre to any other restaurant whose cuisine is similar to the cuisine offered by the tenant [referenced in the use clause]"

Between the use clause and the restrictive covenant, this tenant enjoyed a near monopoly on eat-in, take out or delivery service. The possible exception may be various styles of Asian food. Due to an overlapping grocery anchor restriction, the landlord was also restricted in leasing to food related businesses not deemed as restaurants. Consequently, the landlord was severely handcuffed in their leasing efforts and had to turn away many able and willing tenants resulting in a sustained loss of revenue and ultimately a loss in value when they sold the property. The purchaser simply used the tenant's restrictive as a negotiation point on the price.

Other items to consider when negotiating a restrictive covenant and asking your lawyer to draft a restrictive covenant clause:

- The clause should be personal to the tenant.
- The clause should only apply while the tenant is in full and continuous occupation of the space. No landlord wants a tenant who has 'gone dark' to continue the merchandising in the balance of the property.
- The clause should only apply if the tenant is not in breach or default of the lease (also please see the section on a tenant's continuous breach conditions).
- The clause should be removed or at least suspended if the tenant is on any

form of rent relief. Rent relief is the antithesis for the reason for an exclusivity clause.

While a restrictive covenant should be avoided, if it must be given as part of the negotiation these concepts allow the landlord to retain as much control as possible.

We'll finish this section by noting that both the use clause and the restrictive covenant are directly linked in how they should be structured. If the landlord has inherited poorly worded use clauses and/or restrictive covenants, they should look for every opportunity to restructure each clause.

IN SUMMARY

The use clause is vital to proper merchandising , overall maximization of sales at the property and tenant harmony.

The use clause should detail products, merchandise and services; not general concepts.

The use clause should be subdivided into Primary, Ancillary and Common uses.

A restrictive or exclusivity covenant is a tenant benefit clause that should be avoided.

Percentage rent is the quid pro quo to an exclusivity clause

Restrictive covenants should be tied to the landlord's business of leasing and limited to the tenant's primary use.

Chapter 9
Tenant Benefit Clauses™

'Some Tenant Benefit Clauses can produce a compounding and cascading effect on the landlord'

A Tenant Benefit Clause is any clause in the lease that is solely beneficial to the tenant.

At first glance the landlord may say that these are reasonable considerations in a supplier (landlord) customer (tenant) relationship. The rationale is that since the lease is favored to the landlord, it is reasonable to expect the tenant to negotiate clauses into the lease that benefit the tenant. In fact, anyone working for the tenant should vigorously negotiate for these types of clauses.

However, lets add to the definition: A tenant benefit clause is any clause in the lease that is solely and unilaterally beneficial to the tenant; thereby transferring _all the risk_ related to the item in the clause to the Landlord.

Overall, a well constructed lease provides a balance of risk between the parties and across the property. Tenant benefit clauses don't do this because the point of the clause is to eliminate the tenant's risk in a certain area of the operation of the property and/or the tenant's own business.

So what are the different types of Tenant Benefit Clauses?

Here are a few of the most common:

- A restrictive or exclusive use covenant,
- A co-tenancy clause,
- An option to terminate,
- An option to go dark or cease operations,
- Limits on the Landlord's ability to lease without benefiting the tenant, such as a "most favored" clause, and
- Renewal options.

The last one might surprise you but once you read chapter 7, Negotiating Renewal

Clauses, you'll agree that a renewal or lease term extension clause fits the definition of a tenant benefit clause.

You can also read more about restrictive or exclusive use clauses in chapter 8.

There is a difference between tenant benefit clauses and clauses we call Trap Door™ clauses, with the latter being clauses that on casual reading give the impression of one thing, but can also be interpreted a different way. Trap door clauses are intended to trip up the unsuspecting. The landlord should never draft trap door clauses into the lease for their own benefit and should also be on the look out for potential trap door clauses proposed by the tenant. We discuss these trap door clauses in more detail in the next chapter.

The party with the negotiating power will dictate if tenant benefit clauses are placed, or remain, on the table. When considering these clauses, the landlord must use their judgment to determine the amount of risk they want to assume to conclude the transaction.

However, there are two very important considerations to negotiating all tenant benefit clauses.

1. Mitigating Overall Risk to the Landlord
2. Re-trading Risk Between the Parties

Mitigating Overall Risk

Some tenant benefit clauses can produce a compounding and cascading effect against the landlord, such as having a number of overlapping co-tenancy, termination or go dark clauses. The landlord needs to carefully consider if granting the clause will cause unintended consequences, and negotiate to remove or minimize those issues. Careful drafting of the clauses is also important so the impact of the transferred risk is defined as narrowly as possible. For example, an exclusive use clause needs to be narrowly defined so the landlord retains as much control as possible for the merchandising and leasing of the property.

Re-trading Risk

Any time a tenant requests a tenant benefit clause, the landlord should recognize that the risk has been transferred only to the landlord. Therefore, if the landlord is inclined to accept the concept of the tenant's request for the clause, it is entirely reasonable to negotiate any or all of the following:

- placing conditions on the enactment of the tenant benefit clause, such as thresholds, timing, cure periods, etc.,
- limit the consequences if the clause is enacted,
- re-introduce clauses/ concepts the landlord previously agreed to step-downs or deletions to,
- obtaining a monetary consideration via an increase in the basic rent, or
- trading one tenant benefit clause for another, if there are requests for more than one.

Here is a further look at some of the more common tenant benefit clauses.

Co-Tenancy Clauses

There are essentially two types of co-tenancy clauses. The first is a co-tenancy clause tied to the opening or re-opening of the development or expansion, re-merchandising, etc. The second type of co-tenancy clause is related to the on-going occupation of the property by either types of merchandise, named tenants, or overall occupancy or a combination of these.

Opening Co-Tenancy

The tenant obviously wants some form of assurance that the project will be successful. As a result, the tenant may want to know that the anchor tenant(s) will open on-time and may also tie in other tenants either by name, style or an overall percentage.

In granting the clause the landlord should only agree to those items in their direct control. For example, the landlord should agree to a number of leases or area leased, not open. The reason is that the landlord can use reasonable efforts to ensure the tenant opens on a specific date, but it is typically only in the tenant's power to dictate the premises construction schedule, the arrival of inventory, receipt of permits, etc. The landlord shouldn't assume risk for those things beyond its direct control. The actual leasing of the property is within the control of the Landlord.

The other issue with tying the clause to 'stores open,' is that the landlord can inadvertently create their own issue. This can happen if, as a result of the property not meeting the 'opening requirement', the tenant can also delay it's own opening. In effect, it creates a circular reference. And it happens, unfortunately.

The consequence of the landlord not meeting the opening co-tenancy requirement should be limited to a monetary concession rather than a delayed opening or termination; and it should be limited to a temporary adjustment to the basic rent only. Operating costs and tenant specific charges should still apply because the related expenses will be incurred notwithstanding.

The landlord should also refrain from any co-tenancy that names specific tenants by name (either their legal corporate name or their trade name). There are many reasons for this.

The landlord should also limit the time of the reduced rent either using a period of time as a maximum or unless some other trigger is met, such as a certain sales volume. While the tenant can be expected to object to this because it is contrary to the reason for them asking for the clause in the first place, it is reasonably possible that the tenant will be successful notwithstanding the co-tenancy not being met.

In a phased development or a partial redevelopment, the co-tenancy should only apply to the specific phase or area of the development rather than the entire project. The obvious reason for this is that the landlord doesn't want to inadvertently create an on-going co-tenancy or set up a punitive situation. For example, if the tenant is in an early stage of the a multi-phase development that will ultimately constitute 45% of the entire project, the landlord doesn't want to agree to a 75% occupancy of the entire project rather than 75% of the specific phase.

Fortunately, an opening co-tenancy has relatively limited impact over the life of the property as it is somewhat fixed in time around the opening of the project. Care should be taken in drafting the clause however, so as not to inadvertently create a perpetual co-tenancy requirement.

Here is a real world example. The tenant, a large drug store, was the anchor tenant for a new development. The wording in the opening co-tenancy clause gave the tenant the ability to do <u>any of the following</u> if the co-tenancy requirement was not met:

1. Reduce the minimum rent by 50%,
2. Not operate the store (a "Go Dark" clause) until the co-tenancy requirement was met. Ostensibly, the wording seemed to protect the tenant from opening immediately after construction was complete if the co-tenancy was not met, and
3. Terminate the lease.

The way the clause was worded, the tenant wasn't obligated to pick one of the three; but could enact them together or sequentially. For example, the tenant could choose to go dark and not open and reduce the rent by 50% at the same time.

The landlord/developer was obligated to use 'best efforts' secure leases with both a medical clinic and a medical lab. Notwithstanding a vigorous leasing campaign aimed at attracting those specific uses, the property opened without the co-tenancy requirements in place.

The anchor tenant maintains that the clause simply stated that those uses were to be secured and since there wasn't a timeline for those deals to be completed prior to opening, the tenant interpreted the clause to be both an opening and continuous operating co-tenancy clause.

This is a major concern for that landlord as most leases in the property also contain ongoing co-tenancy clauses relative to the anchor space. This anchor effectively controls the investment in the shopping centre due to the co-tenancy clause wording.

While there may be legal room to argue the fine points of the clause in court, the process will be expensive and an outcome in the landlord's favor is not assured.

On-Going Co-Tenancy

A tenant in a new or established property may also request a co-tenancy provision for the entire term of their lease. The argument is the same as for an opening co-tenancy – the tenant is relying on the success of the overall property.

Again, the tenant may request that the provision be tied to certain tenants being in the property, a certain percentage of the property being leased (and open), etc.

The landlord needs to carefully review any provision that spans several years. In addition to the same considerations required for an opening co-tenancy; here are some other things the landlord should negotiate.

If the landlord agrees to provide a co-tenancy, it should be time limited. For example it may only be effective during the first three years of the term while the tenant becomes established.

The landlord should carefully consider both the historic vacancy at the property and the anticipated lease expires that coincide with the requesting tenant's term – or the time limit. This allows the landlord to negotiate from a position of knowing its potential risk to granting the provision.

Likewise, the landlord should look to see if granting the co-tenancy sets up a cascading effect with co-tenancy provisions in other leases.

The co-tenancy clause should exclude vacancy caused by store closures due to renovations and relocations.

In a multi-phase and/or a multi-building development it is important to limit the area to which the co-tenancy applies. Likewise, it is important to exclude the damage and destruction provisions from triggering the co-tenancy.

Here is a real life example. In 2013 an arson fire completely destroyed a building in a 96% occupied, five building shopping centre. The affected building housed approximately 20% of the tenants by number and area.

Other tenants in the property had co-tenancy agreements that permitted them to reduce their rent or terminate their leases if the total occupancy fell to less than 85%, by number or area. While the landlord's insurance provisions covered loss of income from the destroyed building, it did not include consequential revenue loss due to the business decisions to provide the other tenants with co-tenancy clauses.

Although some tenants attempted to rely on the 85% co-tenancy provision and reduce their rent; the leases excluded the fire from triggering the co-tenancy clause and the landlord's income was protected.

It is also a good idea to limit the tenant's ability to enact the provision to an actual and demonstrable reduction in the tenant's sales as a direct result of the loss of the co-tenancy.

Using the concept of re-trading risk, the landlord can also introduce a quid pro quo in exchange for granting a co-tenancy provision.

Once again, the use of the question "why?" is important. In the vast majority of time, the tenant is requesting the co-tenancy to protect its ability to generate sales. Therefore, rather than providing the tenant with an option to terminate the lease if the provision is enacted, the more appropriate response is a reduction in the minimum rent. But what if the Landlord does something that has the possibility of increasing the tenant's sales? Those may include an expansion, the addition of a high profile tenant, a general mall refurbishment, the additional of other asset classes to the property (ie: residential), etc.

A natural counter to a co-tenancy clause is a request to adjust the rent in some form when there is a significant change in conditions to the property.

Naturally, a tenant will point out that the landlord will receive percentage rent, if it is in the lease. If it is not in the lease, now may be a time to introduce it. However, financiers tend to discount percentage rent so it is not as important as being able to increase the basic rent due to any of these conditions.

This type of a clause is a tough pill for many retailers to swallow because it is not very common. While we believe this is a clause that should be in every lease, each landlord should determine if there will be a significant event during the term of the lease and either insert it or remove it as needed. We've included the concept here to demonstrate how to insert the concept into the negotiation. This type of clause can also be inserted if the tenant requests any amendments to the original lease or an assignment.

The landlord can make it easier for the tenant to digest this provision by specifically defining what is a change in condition that triggers a change in the basic rent and if the change is known at the time of the initial negotiation. For this reason we advocate a percentage increase rather than an open ended statement about an increase in rent "to be negotiated."

Options to Terminate or Cease Operations

These types of options are different than a co-tenancy only inasmuch as the tenant's ability to exercise the option is tied to something other than a certain percentage of the property being leased, or certain tenants being in the property. An option to terminate or cease operations is akin to a "get out of jail" free card in Monopoly®.

This type of clause, if broadly worded, gives the tenant ultimate control and the landlord assumes 100% of the risk without any control.

Even if the landlord conditions the exercising of either of these two different options with certain events – such as sales performance – the landlord has no direct control over the events leading to the exercise. For example, a store can manipulate its inventory to

166

achieve a reduction in volume in order to exercise the clause, if the clause is tied to a minimum sales performance.

Landlords should object to these types of clauses arguing that the point of the lease is positive and proactive. The parties should not be contemplating 'what if' options. Smart merchants will still demand the option.

If the landlord does have to provide either an option to terminate or an option to cease operations, the landlord must mitigate the financial and business risks in the following manner:

Option to Terminate

Aside from placing conditions on when a tenant may exercise the option, such as a minimum sales volume, only after X number of years of the term, the death of the principle owner (in the case of a single owner specialty operation); the landlord will want significant notice before the lease is terminated to allow the landlord to find a replacement tenant.

The landlord also wants repayment of the unamortized portion of any inducements paid since they were provided in anticipation of the successful completion of the lease as well as the unamortized portion of any costs incurred in the leasing (including commissions and legal costs).

If the landlord incurs any costs requested by the tenant in the build-out of the space at the onset of the lease, these should be recaptured, if possible.

Any other beneficial clauses, such as an exclusivity or restrictive covenant should end at the time of the notice. The reason for this is that the landlord may end up replacing the outgoing tenant with another like tenant. However, the landlord shouldn't assume that it will be in the same location or only occur once the departing tenant has left. Once the departing tenant has made it known they no longer want a relationship with this location, the landlord must concern themselves with the longer term impact on their property. It is important that this concept of the termination of these types of clauses occur before the end of the lease is clearly spelled out in the clause. It is rarely captured in the drafting of these clauses.

Option to Cease Operations

Landlords tend to favor this type of clause over an option to terminate since the landlord still receives an income steam. This clause allows the tenant to cease operations but still enjoy the lease and the space.

A dark premises in the property can be detrimental to the image and leasing of the property. It can also hurt other tenant's sales. Therefore, in addition to the conditions for an option to terminate; the landlord needs the option to terminate the lease at any time after the tenant has provided notice that it will cease operations. This allows the landlord to re-lease the premises, turn the lights back on and have an operating premises in addition to obtaining the rent.

Most Favored Clause

This is a term many have not heard before because it is our term for a new type of clause requested by knowledgeable, brand name tenants.

The concept of a most favored clause, as portrayed by the tenant, is that the owner won't act negatively to the tenant as compared to other tenants. The tenant's lawyer will submit broad wording that upon closer examination, shows its true intent. This intent means that the landlord won't negotiate any clauses contained in the tenant's lease on more favorable terms with any other tenant during the lease term. For example, if the tenant's lease has a three mile radius clause and the owner agrees to a two mile radius for another tenant, the original tenant radius will now be two miles.

Obviously, there are many significant issues with this type of clause. Essentially, the tenant who has this clause is perpetually in a position of negotiating their lease terms for the duration of the lease, plus they obtain the benefit of concessions that may only be available to a stronger tenant.

The tenant requesting this type of clause may introduce it near the end of the negotiation as the owner counters other requests. The tact the tenant may use could be as simple as saying: "Ok, we have given more on these points than we normally would. You beat us up Mr./Ms. Landlord, but we both want to conclude this lease; we just don't want you to offer the next merchant more than you are will to give us, so let's agree you won't do that, OK? That is a reasonable request and you wouldn't do that, would you?" The last question is made more as a statement making it a rhetorical question to which they don't expect an answer. Based on this conversation, they instruct their lawyer to insert the most favored clause.

Be wary of all tenant submitted clauses that use words such as equitable, equally, etc. Pay particular attention to these clauses. Ideally, they shouldn't be included in the lease.

The best negotiating defense to this request is to simply note that it is unworkable and deny it with a "positive no". It is unworkable because the landlord would have to divulge confidential information from another lease in order to comply. Something the landlord simply cannot do.

Tenant Benefit Clause Claw-back

The landlord should always retain the ability to claw-back or terminate tenant benefit clauses if the tenant doesn't uphold its end of the contract. The lease document should contain specific wording that the tenant benefit clauses end if the tenant goes into default of the lease.

Likewise, the landlord needs to carefully review the lease for tenant benefit clauses should the tenant request any amendments to the lease, assignment or subletting. The landlord can then introduce the termination of these as part of those negotiations.

IN SUMMARY

Tenant Benefit Clauses transfer all the risk to the landlord, by their very nature.

While they should be avoided in the negotiation, the landlord must add conditions to the tenant's ability to enact these clauses to mitigate that risk and should retain an ability to claw-back the clauses.

Some Tenant Benefit Clauses can have a cascading effect on other leases leading to catastrophic consequences for the unwary landlord, so extreme care must be taken to carefully analyze each potential concession.

Chapter 10
Trap Door Clauses™

It is the fool who thinks he cannot be fooled.   **Joey Skaggs**

A trap door clause is any clause that can be read in more than one way. Typically, a trap door clause results from either a deliberate attempt to mislead the other party via ambiguous wording or context; or they arise from sloppy wordsmithing. The latter is due to either too much - or too little - verbiage and can be caught up in legalese.

Whether it is an attempt to mislead or bad lease crafting, trap door clauses rely on two basic negotiating elements:

1. both parties not being absolutely clear on the intent of the clause and the agreement between them; and

2. the party on the receiving, or granting, end of the clause assumes the meaning intended based on a preconceived notion or prejudice.

Here is a real life example of a trap door clause. Given the people involved, the reason for the clause being drafted into the in the lease in the manner described, the reason the trap door clause came to be was more than likely due to a combination of poor wording of the clause, interpreted by people involved in the property long after the initial negotiation and lease drafting, rather than a deliberate attempt to mislead the landlord. However, you can see how the issue arose as well as the consequences in this example.

The lease involved a sophisticated brand name tenant and an intelligent, experienced landlord. The clause pertained to the allocation of real estate taxes to the tenant premises and was drafted by the tenant, rather than the landlord, so it was 'off standard' to the landlord's lease form.

A paraphrase of the lease wording was that the tenant would pay as its portion of the total property taxes, those taxes applicable to the tenant's premises in proportion to the total tax bill and the taxes on the land under the tenant premises.

On the surface, this wording seems common and reasonable. To the landlord it seemed that the wording approximated the wording in their own lease.

Other points to know and consider:

- The tenant's premises represented about 10% of the total GLA.
- The assessed value was based using the income approach.
- The municipality in which the property was located determined the property taxes based on the assessed value of the property and (arbitrarily) split the total tax bill between the land value and the value of the improvements on the basis of approximately 30% of the total bill was deemed to be on the land and 70% on the improvements.
- The tenant's per square foot rent was about 35% of the average rent in the balance of the property as they were a sub-anchor, and
- The building occupied about 25% of the total property area, with the balance being parking lot and landscaping.

How would you determine the tenant's share of the taxes?

The landlord sent the tenant a bill for 10% of the total taxes.

Since this chapter is about trap door clauses, you have already surmised that the tenant objected to the bill based on the wording in the lease. Here were their arguments:

- The lease provided that the tenant would pay its portion of those taxes applicable to the tenant's premises.

While the landlord read that to mean a proportionate share of the total tax bill (thus 10%), the tenant argued that since the tax bill was based on the assessed value of the property using the income approach, then it should be the tenant's rent assessment in proportion to the total tax (please read the chapter on realty taxes to have a full understanding of the method the tenant suggested). Since the tenant had a lower per square foot rent than the balance of the property, the value assessment on a per square foot basis was less than the balance of the centre and far less than 10% of the total.

But that wasn't the tenant's only argument.

- Since the tax bill was separated into both land and improvements the tenant's portion above should be calculated only on the 70% of the overall tax bill (the improvements portion) as that represented the tenant's premises, and

- The land portion of the total tax bill should be based on a calculation of the tenant's premises area in the numerator and the total property land mass (including the parking lot and landscape) in the denominator. Their argument was that the lease specifically stated the tax on the land under the tenant's premises. Their interpretation of the clause included the unwritten word "ONLY". This had the effect of dramatically reducing the tenant's portion of almost 1/3 of the total tax bill.

Combined these created a significant shortfall to the landlord. Here is a simplified look at the effect of the landlord's billing v the tenant's calculation.

Landlord's bill: 10% of 100% of the bill

Tenant's interpretation of the clause:

Tenant's premises portion was 35% (their rent) of 10% (their area) of 70% of the total tax bill (representing the improvements portion of the tax bill) = 2.45% of the total applied to the improvements; plus

Tenant's portion of the land was $10/400^1$ X 30% of the total taxes = 0.75% of the total tax bill.

Tenant's interpretation of its total tax obligation, as a percentage of the total tax bill, was 3.2%.

Note[1]: 400 represents the tenant's premise area to the total land mass since the overall building occupied 1/4 of the total area of the property.

Quite a difference in cash flow between a 10% recovery and a 3.2% recovery.

Now lets take that one step further and look at the impact on value of that 6.8% slippage. At a 7% capitalization rate every dollar in slippage equates to $14.29 in lost value! That is almost **$143,000** in value for every $10,000 the landlord didn't collect on the tax bill from this tenant.

In addition to the direct financial impact, the landlord and tenant had a strained relationship during to the discussions that followed, which included threats of court action by both parties.

For these obvious reasons we advise our clients to both be on the look out for trap door clauses as well as to never engage in putting trap door clauses into the lease themselves. No one likes the idea of being hoodwinked and will remember it for a long time.

So what are the common trap door clauses?

The correct answer is; "It Depends."

Because trap door clauses occur by either sloppy lease drafting or by specific malicious intent, they can occur in any clause in the lease where the interpretation can differ from the language. A simple misplaced comma can have a significant impact.

The best way to protect the landlord is the old adage Say what you mean, mean what you say and then clearly, and concisely, write down the intent of the article EXACTLY as it should be read. If the landlord suspects the wording can be read in different ways, they should immediately point to the potential issue and demand clarification as to the meaning. That clarification should be specifically drafted into the lease.

Back to our example. The landlord and tenant eventually came to a mutual agreement on how the tax bill should be allocated to the tenant. That agreement resulted in a billing between the two interpretations. More importantly, the two parties also committed the revised agreement to paper by way of a lease amending agreement. If the landlord discovers a real or potential trap door clause, the clause should be discussed and the lease amended to eliminate future interpretation issues.

IN SUMMARY

A Trap Door Clause is *any clause* in the lease that can be read and interpreted more than one way.

Trap Door Clauses can occur inadvertently or with intent. In either case, the landlord needs to be vigilant in making sure any are identified and resolved during the negotiation and, ideally, before the lease is executed.

One of the most prevalent reasons trap door clauses occur is the assumption by one or both parties that the intent is clear and can only be interpreted one way.

Real and potential Trap Door Clauses, once identified, should be clarified and the lease amended to remove confusion over the term of the lease.

182

Chapter 11
Non-Standard Issues
with Standard Clauses

**Any concessions to 'standard' wording
typically results in the landlord assuming
more risk.**

BOILERPLATE *(noun)*

- *any of the standard clauses or sections
  of a legal document*
                        -   Webster's

On balance, the lease is generally divided
into three sections (excluding schedules,
exhibits and appendixes). Those are:

1. Proactive clauses. These include
   clauses concerning positive actions

and includes the business terms of the transaction.

2. Negative Clauses. These include what happens if the positive actions do not occur, such as default provisions, bankruptcy, etc.
3. Standard legal or boilerplate clauses. These are clauses one expects to see from one lease to another.

In this chapter we will look at some of the 'standard' clauses that tenant negotiate, how their typical step down requests to the standard wording may affect the landlord and how the landlord should negotiate those to minimize risk. This is not an exhaustive list, since every word in every lease is open for negotiation. Instead we will focus on some of the clauses that are negotiated most often that have the most impact on the landlord.

These are:

- Reasonableness
- Mutual indemnity
- Self insurance
- Damage and destruction
- Default Provisions

Reasonableness

A fairly common request by tenants is that the landlord act reasonably in all it actions relative to the lease. While you intend to generally act in a reasonable manner, the lease does provide areas where the landlord may be unreasonable and arbitrary. While this is more of a legal test, and you should consult your attorney concerning the various tests and consequences of being, and proving being, 'reasonable', it does have business consequences and assumed risks.

The best solution is to never grant a carte blanche agreement to act reasonably in all circumstances. In the alternative, ask the tenant why they are requesting the clause and to provide examples, then draft wording in only those clauses that you are comfortable with the concept.

Mutual or Reciprocal Indemnity

Another common request is that the landlord will indemnify the tenant, just as the landlord seeks an indemnity from the tenant. The request is almost always phrased this way too.

The issue is that the landlord is assuming a much greater implied and financial risk than the indemnity provided by the tenant, so it really isn't reciprocal or mutual.

Most leases provide that the tenant will indemnify and hold harmless the landlord for the actions of the tenant, and certain others, within the tenant's premises or in the conduct of the tenant's business. Therein is the problem, the tenant's premises is contained and within the tenant's control.

Conversely, the landlord has to contend with the balance of the property, with free access to the public. The tenant is asking the landlord to assume disproportionate risk, given the scope of the difference in size and control between the two parties.

Depending on how the mutual indemnification clause is worded, it can also be deemed a trap door clause (see the chapter on trap door clauses for more information about these) because the tenant could argue that the cost of insurance for the common area and insurance deductibles don't apply to them due to the concept of indemnification by the landlord.

The best counter to this request is to deny it, point to the disparity and note that both parties carry insurance.

Self Insurance

A large, brand name tenant may request self insurance on some or all the items it is required to insurance. Self insurance is where the tenant assumes all the financial risk for a casualty. A simple example of self insurance may be where the tenant pays out of pocket for the replacement a broken glass door or window, rather than having plate glass insurance.

Aside from the example (because the cost is relatively minor) self insurance is fraught with problems, but the landlord may permit it to complete the transaction. Here are the potential pitfalls and potential solutions.

Typically, the landlord wants to be named on the tenant's insurance, and as evidence of the coverage the landlord obtains a certificate of insurance from the tenant's insurance company. If the tenant is self insuring, the landlord needs to ensure that the lease wording is expanded to include that the landlord is still covered under the self insurance and that the tenant will provide separate acknowledgement of that concept.

Another pitfall is if the lease is assigned to another company. The assignee may not have the financial depth to pay out on a self insured claim. This may include an assignment to a subsidiary of the original tenant. The insurance section of the lease is often overlooked when considering assignments. Bottom line is the landlord will incur additional management expense (and potential exposure) administering to the tenant's self insurance. The landlord should include a check of the insurance provisions in the lease if an assignment is contemplated and revert to the standard lease wording as a condition of the landlord's consent to the assignment if needed.

If the tenant incurs several significant self insurance claims it may not have the ability to pay a claim. Likewise, the net worth of the tenant may suffer at some point for some other reason, such as the closure of a division, reorganization, liquidity issues, etc. The landlord's best defense in both these cases is to condition the tenant's ability to self insure on the value of the company being at least equal to the same amount at the start of the lease. Ideally, this should be stated numerically in the lease rather than just outlining the concept. Should the value of the tenant drop below a certain level then, the standard lease wording would apply and the tenant would need to insure through an insurance company.

And here is a big one.

Would allowing self insurance by a tenant be compatible with the provisions of the mortgage or the landlord's own insurance? Generally, speaking many lenders and insurance companies do not have an issue with limited self insurance provisions, such as self insurance on plate glass. It is important to know the obligations under both the mortgage and the insurance documents before negotiating or agreeing to self insurance provisions.

Damage and Destruction

The landlord can inadvertently assume more than the intended risk with modifications to these clauses. In addition, the landlord needs to be careful when crafting the property template lease – another reason not to accept an off the shelf lease form.

There are two scenarios when considering modifications to damage and destruction clauses. The first is damage to the tenant's premises. The second is damage to the balance of the property.

Damage to the tenant's own premises is pretty straight forward; however, the landlord should resist requests for a required relocation of the tenant's business, for a first right of refusal to release the rebuilt premises or to maintain the existing rent after reconstruction.

Since the tenant will negotiate this in the initial lease, the landlord would have to make a number of assumptions in granting any of these requests. For example, would the landlord have available space in the property for a required relocation? Will this be the right tenant in the right place after reconstruction? Will the space be rebuilt as is? What would be the net cost to the landlord for reconstruction and would the tenant's existing rent be appropriate at that time.

Damage to the shopping centre is a little different and depends on the type of development. A tenant may request the ability to terminate its lease or seek a substantial rent reduction for damage to the 'Shopping Centre' as it is defined in the lease. However, that may not always be appropriate.

If, for example, the property is comprised of a number of buildings, one of those buildings may be destroyed with no affect on the tenant's business located in another building. Landlords want to avoid placing themselves in the position of the property emptying out when it is still viable as an operating concern.

Default Provisions

There are provisions in the lease when agreements are not upheld. Many tenants automatically request adjustments to these as a matter of course. The adjustments most requested pertain to the time to cure a breach of the agreement.

The first inclination concerning these requests is to counter with a resounding "NO". After all, it is the tenant that has brought forward the breach; however, there are a number of reasonable explanations for a request for a longer time to cure a breach, particularly in a large company, so it is up to the landlord to determine the flexibility they want to offer.

But, there are a few types of breach that should never warrant a longer cure period than the landlord originally placed in the lease. The following types of breach should be excluded from any longer cure periods the landlord grants:

- Risk to the landlord's title in the property
- Risk to the landlord's insurance

- Risk to the landlord's mortgage
- Risk of personal injury or damage to others
- Environmental Risk
- Risk to the landlord's reputation
- Breach of authority or regulatory direction (ie: Health & Fire Department directions or Zoning bylaws)
- A failure to pay any form of rent, particularly big ticket items such as property taxes if paid in a lump sum
- Any illegal activity

The risk to the landlord is substantially greater than the risk to the tenant for not having the additional cure period.

IN SUMMARY

Any requests to step down 'standard' wording typically results in the landlord assuming more risk.

The landlord shouldn't have to act reasonably in all situations.

There is no such thing as a mutual indemnification in a commercial lease.

Self Insurance requests should be considered very carefully and in consultation with the landlord's own insurance company, lenders, etc.

Certain types of defaults require an immediate cure by the tenant.

Chapter 12
Handling Assignments and Subtenancies

The risk profile of the covenant is about to change.

Once an assignment or sublet is completed
the landlord is no longer dealing with the
person or entity they originally negotiated
the lease with, so it is important to carefully
consider the assignment and subleasing
provisions at the time of the original lease
negotiation.

Two caveats to the previous paragraph.
Although the original tenant is still the
responsible party in a sublease situation, the
daily operation of the merchant is in the
hands of someone else. Therefore, there is an

extra party involved in the lease that the landlord must consider.

Likewise, a franchise operation may result in either a sublet or assignment of the original lease. Special considerations are required to protect the landlord when leasing to a franchising tenant, which we will also review.

Assignment

Typically, the landlord needs to consent to any assignment because the act of the assignment means the tenant is changing. An assignment can arise from a number of situations. Each may bring a different nuance to how the landlord will negotiate its consent. The two important underlying concepts of an assignment are:

    a. the lease contract is being transferred from one party to another, and
    b. the original tenant (assignor) is putting forward an entity to 'step into the shoes' of the assignor.

A fairly basic concept, but with these come two implications.

The first is that the new tenant (assignee) receives the benefits of the previously negotiated lease contract. All the previous tenant's negotiating strength is transferred and the landlord has limited ability at the time of the assignment to insert more negotiating strength. So it is important to ensure the landlord retains the negotiating strength during the initial lease negotiations, when discussing this clause.

How is this done? The first step is to require that the landlord's written consent is needed. The tenant may counter that the landlord's consent can't be unreasonably withheld. While it is always preferable to not provide this wording, if it is required then the landlord must spell out when withholding consent would be reasonable. The withholding of consent would be reasonable if it included, amongst other things, the assignee has a poor history, the financial covenant of the assignee is not to the landlord's standards, the reputation of the assignee is questionable, a trading in the landlord's real estate by assigning within a period immediately after commencement of the term or before the expiration of the term, a change in the rent structure, and if the assignor does not remain on the lease as an indemnifier or co-covenantor. The landlord needs to have wording in the assignment clause that allows the landlord to request information about the assignment and the assignee in order to assess the landlord's ability to provide consent. The specifics of what information is required is not drafted into the lease because that information may change over the term of the lease.

The next is to insert wording into all tenant benefit clauses (see chapter 9) that makes the clause personal to the original tenant, so they can be removed at the time of an assignment.

The landlord should retain the ability to change the rent structure upon an assignment. There are many reasons for this. The tenant risk profile may be changing. The landlord and tenant now have a sales history that the assignee will benefit from, whereas in the original lease this may not have been known. If the original tenant was paying percentage rent, the assignee may not and the landlord will want to protect this income. And the lapse of time may warrant an increase in the same manner as a renewal option warrants an increase due to inflation.

Speaking of renewal options, we favor using the same rent formulas to calculate the new rent resulting from an assignment as used in the renewal clause discussed in Chapter 7.

A carefully crafted Use Clause is also beneficial during an assignment, because the assignee must conduct the exact same business as the original tenant. Even though the landlord may permit a change in the trade name as part of the assignment, it is important for the merchandising of the property that the premise use remains the same. If the new tenant requests a change in the use or an expansion in the use, the landlord gains negotiating strength because the assignor and assignee are both requesting a modification to the original agreement. This 'opens' the lease to further negotiation by the landlord, or the landlord may also simply say the lease is the lease and there is no option to change the lease at the time of the assignment. Please see Chapter 8 for more information about a well structured use clause.

The second implication of the assignment is that the risk associated with the original transaction has changed simply because the covenant of the operating tenant has changed. Granted it could be improved in a case where a specialty tenant wants to assign the lease to a brand name operator, for example; but this rarely happens.

The assignor is telling the landlord that the entity taking over the lease is as good or better than they are as a tenant. More often than not however, the assignee is an entity the landlord knows nothing or very little about. As a result, the landlord must protect themselves during the initial lease negotiation, with the original tenant, for a change in the risk profile associated with an assignment.

The best way to accomplish this is to secure additional comfort regarding the covenant as a condition of an assignment. The two preferred methods are to have the assignee provide a covenantor's agreement and/or a letter of credit; and have the assignor continue to indemnify and co-covenant the assignee. These should provisions should be non-negotiable from the landlord's perspective.

Of course the landlord can also carry the ultimate big stick and have a standard clause in the lease that permits the landlord to terminate the lease if the tenant wants to assign it. As you can imagine, this type of clause is not popular with tenants. Those with significant leasing strength simple delete it, while others state that the landlord can't act to terminate the lease if the tenant withdraws the assignment request.

Why would a landlord want this type of termination ability in the assignment clause?

The philosophical reason is that the lease negotiated is personal to the tenant, as we discussed. If the tenant wants to interject another (typically unknown) party into the lease, then the landlord should be free to negotiate freely with the other party or any other party simply because it is the landlord's property and the landlord should retain control over whom they decide to do business with, rather than the tenant.

The more practical reasons are:

- The assignment may be the result of the tenant wanting out of a bad situation by selling to an unwitting or misguided entity. If the landlord allowed the assignment, then the landlord may be perpetuating a bad situation. It may be a tough recognition by all parties that the specific merchandising or use concept simply does not work at that property.
- The clause protects the landlord in case of an unauthorized assignment of the lease, that the landlord has not consented to in the first place. It gives control of the premises back to the landlord. The mere presence of the option to terminate in case of an assignment - requested or not – is also intended to put the tenant parties on notice that there is a potential and

sizable risk to the business and tenancy if there is an unauthorized assignment.

-   The assignment may also be a condition of a refinancing wherein the lease is pledged as security for the loan. This gives the lender control over the lease. Because loans tend to have preferred debtor rights under various bankruptcy laws, the landlord may not want to lessen its rights in its real estate and elect to terminate the lease instead.

Large Corporation Assignments

Brand name tenants regularly request an amendment to the assignment clause wherein the landlord's consent is <u>not</u> required for an assignment of the lease to certain entities. Generally speaking these assignments are related to either the corporate structure of the company, such as an assignment of the lease to an affiliate or subsidiary of the tenant or as a result of corporate restructuring or financing. They can also relate to a share sale or an asset sale.

The landlord must be aware that each of these can mean the covenant of the tenant changes, sometimes dramatically. Here are a few examples:

A Sale

A national chain with a superb covenant wishes to sell a few of it's locations and has found a buyer of the one location in the landlord's property. The covenant changes from a credit tenant to a specialty tenant as a result. This can also trigger co-tenancy agreements, producing a cascading effect on the property, so please read chapter 9 concerning the negotiation of co-tenancy agreements. To mitigate this risk, the landlord should insist on providing its consent to an assignment if only a few of the tenant's locations are sold. We advise clients to negotiate for as wide a geographic area as possible (ie: all the locations in [*named states, provinces, jurisdictions*] are sold to a single entity), or a majority of the locations, including the landlord's location are sold to a single entity.

Did you also note the nuances in the general concepts?

It is important to note that the buyer is a single entity, otherwise the wording is meaningless because it could still permit a single unit sale. For the same reason, if using the concept of a majority of locations sold, the landlord's location must be one of those locations. Otherwise, the majority of all locations could be sold to one group and the landlord's specific location sold either individually or as part of a sale of a much smaller number of locations. The absence of the reference to the landlord's location as part of the majority sale defeats the protection the landlord wants.

A Re-Organization

The brand name tenant assigns the lease to an affiliate or subsidiary as part of a re-organization. Your lawyer will tell you that you have a new legal entity as a tenant. Thus, the covenant has changed. In some cases the tenant may have created an entity with the only purpose to hold leases. As a result, it only holds liabilities and no assets resulting in virtually no covenant for the landlord. To mitigate this risk, the landlord should insist on two things:

1. that any assignment encompass a majority of the leases to a single related entity. This protects the landlord in case the parent company spins off the subsidiary or affiliate, and
2. that the original or parent company remain as a covenantor after the assignment. This protects the landlord from an assignment to a shell or liability only company.

A Change in the Nature of the Business

A regional brand name tenant intends to grow its business by franchising it's concept. While the brand name remains, the covenant changes after the assignment, from the company and franchisor to the covenant of a franchisee. To protect itself the landlord should never include a franchisee in any type of assignment that can be completed without landlord's consent.

Later in this chapter we discuss the special considerations regarding leasing to and the needed assignment and subleasing negotiation provisions around franchises.

Now lets look at subleases generally.

Subleasing

In a sublease the original tenant is still the responsible party and is the actual tenant; however, the daily operation is conducted by someone else. Therefore, there is an extra party involved in the lease that the landlord must consider.

From the perspective of the initial lease negotiation, the landlord's consent should be required in the same manner as an assignment and the lease wording in the clause will generally include both assignment and subletting together. As a result, most of the comments about assignments apply to subleasing with a few notable exceptions.

The landlord's ability to terminate the lease, change the rent or claw back tenant benefit clauses is removed since the actual tenant under the lease (also known as the 'sublessor' or 'sublandlord' in a subletting situation) is not changing.

Conversely, the landlord doesn't want the tenant to 'trade in its real estate.' Too often landlord's leases are silent on whether or not the tenant can charge the subtenant more rent than the tenant pays the landlord. Some landlords agree to split any incremental rent the tenant receives 50/50. Neither concept seems satisfactory because the tenant is profiting from the landlord's (limited) stock in trade. The landlord should prohibit any type of incremental rent accruing to the tenant.

There are important items that should be discussed at the time of the request to sublease.

Your lawyer may tell you that to be a sublease rather than a de facto assignment, the tenant (sublessor) must reserve a part of the lease to itself. This can be a part of the rent, a part of the premises or part of the term. The most common way to deal with this legal provision, with the least amount of administrative or managerial time and cost, is to make the sublease match the (applicable) term of the lease less one day. This applies to the initial term and during any subsequent renewal periods.

This also means the sublease must be renewed each time the head lease is renewed. We advocate using a new sublease between the sublessor and the subtenant, and sublease consent between the landlord, sublessor and subtenant each time.

The landlord's consent document should include wording that states that accepting rent directly from the subtenant does not amount to an assignment of the lease to the subtenant, nor does it preclude the landlord from seeking any unpaid balance from the tenant. Since this must be very precise wording relative to the laws in your jurisdiction, it is important to have your lawyer construct the appropriate wording.

Franchises

A franchise organization presents unique dynamics to the leasing process. Not the least of which is determining who will actually be the tenant.

Some franchise organizations want to control the space and become the tenant. The franchisor enters into the lease and becomes the tenant, subsequently subleasing to the franchisee. Others prefer to provide real estate advise and services to the franchisee, such as site selection and lease negotiation, but the franchisee itself becomes the tenant. Knowing which concept will be used dictates the negotiating strategy of the landlord.

Franchisor as Tenant

This can seem like it is the most advantageous of the two options. However, it is important to carefully determine the covenant of the actual entity that will be the tenant. Many franchisors legally partition their business into different entities with royalty fee into one entity and leases held in another entity with no actual assets. It is important at the outset of the negotiation to have the franchisor clarify and prove the covenant of the true lessee and, if needed the landlord needs to introduce protections to the covenant such as an indemnification by the parent company, etc.

It is also a prudent business move not to let the franchisor assign the responsibility of paying the rent to the franchisee. The franchisor typically has greater financial resources than the single franchisee.

Most franchisors will request that the landlord's consent requirement is waived for a bona fide franchisee as a subtenant. This is fairly common and is acceptable since the franchisee is vetted in the franchising process and the franchisor remains on the lease as the tenant. However, be careful of wording that includes a "sublease or assignment".

When negotiating the initial lease, the franchisor may condition the offer to lease to securing a franchisee within a certain timeframe. The common request is for a 90 day period to find a franchisee. This is also common, but if the landlord agrees to this, the landlord must retain the ability to potentially lease the space to others while the franchisor is attempting to find a franchisee. This clause is often negotiated so that if the landlord finds an alternate tenant (subject to vacant possession), the tenant has a very limited time to waive its condition, such as 48 hours. This type of compromise wording meets the business objectives of both the landlord and the franchisor.

Franchisee as Tenant

This is becoming more common if the franchisor doesn't want to assume the liability of the costs of the lease.

A franchisor may enter into an offer or lease with an added proviso that it can be assigned to a bona fide franchisee of the system without triggering the landlord's options to increase the rent, terminate, charge an administration fee etc.

Don't Make This Real Life Mistake!

Unfortunately, we've seen instances where the tenant is listed in the offer to lease as "to be named" or "a franchisee of XYZ brand". Our lawyers advise us that because one of the two parties to the contract cannot be specifically identified, there is no valid contract. Your lawyer will probably say the same, so insist on having the franchisor named on the offer and/or the lease. The change in the tenant can always be dealt with in the consent to assignment document.

Alternatively to the franchisor securing the space, the franchisee may find the location, start the negotiation and then turn over the final lease negotiation to the franchisor's real estate department; however, the franchise becomes the tenant.

In either case, the covenant the landlord has is with the franchisee and not the franchisor so the landlord must go through their normal vetting process when leasing and secure the covenant with a covenantor's agreement, letter of credit, etc.

A unique dynamic when the franchisee is the tenant is that the landlord gains a brand name tenant; but the control of that brand rests with a third party who is not part of the operating agreement between the landlord and the tenant/franchisee. While this is not a concern where the franchisor is the tenant, and is part of the agreement with the landlord; it does have implications in this case.

Consider the answer to this question. What happens if the tenant loses the franchise? No landlord wants the internationally known burger franchise they negotiated for to become a single location hamburger stand almost overnight.

The implication for the former franchisee can be financially fatal if the former franchisee is required to remove markets, design elements, colours, menus, etc. identifiable to the franchisor and then reconstruct and rebrand as something else. As a result, the landlord will also likely lose a tenant. Moreover, it could have little or nothing to do with the landlord's property because the loss of the franchise agreement may stem from some other aspect of that business arrangement between the franchisee and the franchisor. This too can trigger cascading co-tenancy issues in other leases.

Because the franchise agreement is a third party agreement, the landlord has little recourse in this situation. In fact, because the tenant will continue to be the former franchisee and retains a right to occupy the premises, the landlord and franchisor are both precluded from entering into another lease for that space. This has been the case where the location has been successful but animosity has built between the franchisee and the franchisor.

The best protection for the landlord is to condition the continued tenancy on the tenant being a bona fide franchisee of that specific system. If the tenant loses the franchise, then the landlord can terminate the lease on short notice.

While this may seem like an end game solution where the landlord loses the rent because the landlord terminates the lease, it is no worse a situation than they would likely face. The cost of un-banding, closing for renovations and creating a new business may force the tenant out of business over time with the possibility of a replacement tenant lost. Or the landlord is stuck with a tenant that may not have a brand that contributes to the Story to Sell or the well being of the property as a whole and yet the tenant may also enjoy all the negotiating strength and privileges the brand name tenants could secure in the negotiation (ie: exclusivity, etc.).

More recently, the industry has seen a hybrid of the two types of franchise tenants.

In this case the franchisee is the tenant, but the franchisor retains some control over the space. This is done in the assignment section of the tenant/franchisee's lease and is sometimes referred to as a franchisor's reversionary option.

Here is how the option works.

The tenant is in default of the lease and the landlord notifies the franchisee that it is in breach. The landlord concurrently notifies the franchisor of the breach. The franchisor retains the option to cure the breach and if the franchisor does so, the lease is immediately assigned to the franchisor. The defaulted franchisee is out of the premises and the franchisor becomes the tenant. The franchisor also simultaneously reserves the right to assign the lease, now in the name of the franchisor, to a new bona fide franchisee of the system with such lease still containing the franchisor's reversionary option.

The key elements of granting a franchisor's reversionary option are to keep the franchisor's timeframe to cure the breach the same as contained in the franchisee's lease so any issues don't compound, and not to condition the franchisor to have a replacement franchisee to any period of time, otherwise the franchisor could potentially close the business during the period while they seek a new franchisee/tenant. The landlord wants the breach cured immediately and wants the public to have a seamless experience at the franchise without any undue downtime during the transition.

This type of reversionary option is as close as the landlord may get to having the franchisor as the actual tenant throughout the term. For that reason, we advise our clients to include a reversionary option in the negotiations where the tenant is the franchisee, even if it is not suggested by the franchisor.

 One last word of caution about leasing to a franchise system, irrespective of who the tenant is on the lease.

The landlord should never permit a step down in the lease that allows the tenant to remove its improvements *at its option.* Franchisors build their brand through identification, as well as other things. Trademarks, copyrights and patents, in some cases, protect many design components to the premises. Leaving those improvements in situ does not mean that those rights and protections vest to the landlord or a subsequent tenant.

One unfortunate landlord found this out the hard way when an iconic, free standing building that was purpose built for the fast food tenant became vacant with all improvements, except the tenant's sign, left behind - at the tenant's option. The landlord found a replacement tenant. Shortly after the new tenant opened for business the former tenant demanded the new tenant and the landlord remove all identifiers to avoid consumer confusion, citing their design protections.

The end result was the design elements including the exterior wall finishes, roof line profile, etc. had to be removed and a new design installed. The cost to the landlord and the new tenant was significant in expense, management time and reputation.

IN SUMMARY

An assignment always means a change in the covenant of the tenant and many times an increase in the risk profile.

A subtenancy results in similar concerns for the landlord as an assignment, plus additional issues arise in the management of the lease and the multiple parties involved.

Large corporations will commonly ask for certain situations when the landlord's consent is not required. That request should be considered carefully before being granted and should come with certain exclusions and conditions.

Franchises present their own unique dynamics not the least of which is determining who the tenant really will be.

Chapter 13
Dealing with Ancillary Documents

"It's never over till it's over"
American Proverb

There are a number of ancillary documents that are negotiated between the landlord and the tenant over the period of the relationship. Most of these are straight forward legal documents that outline the changes in the business terms contained in the lease. Some of these are:

I.   Lease amending agreements. Essentially all ancillary documents, with the exception of the original letter of intent and the offer to lease, are lease amending agreements by their very nature. The purpose of the agreement is to modify the original understanding between the parties documented in the lease.

II.   Consent Agreements. These provide one party's consent to a modification of an action under the lease. Most consent agreements tend to also modify the lease provisions and may be referred to as a Consent and Amending Agreement.

III.   Extension Agreements. If you've read the chapter on renewal options you should tend to only have a few extension agreements in your portfolio as you modify how the renewal is completed.

IV.   Indemnity and Covenantor Agreement. This agreement is most often attached to the initial lease but can also be introduced at any time during the term as the negotiation warrants.

Letters of Intent

The purpose of a letter of intent (also known as "LOI") is to move a negotiation forward. Your lawyer may tell you that a letter of intent is non-binding on the parties.

A letter of intent is used by the landlord and their representatives to confirm an initial leasing discussion with a prospective tenant. It may be as simple as a letter, or more formalized as a legal looking document.

Having the tenant counter-sign a letter or document provides both parties with a form of comfort that there is mutual understanding of the discussion to date, even though it may be legally non-binding. It also gives the landlord's representative, if used, an opportunity to discuss the potential transaction with the landlord with some assurance that the final transaction's basic business terms will be close to the ones presented in the letter of intent, subject of course to any counters between the parties.

It is always wise, particularly when dealing with less sophisticated prospects to have the discussion, and then to note in the letter of intent, that the purpose of the letter of intent is simply to outline the framework of the negotiation, subject to a final approval. Unfortunately, when this hasn't occurred there have been times when the prospect feels that the landlord - or whomever is negotiating on behalf of the landlord - has made a binding representation of the lease terms. While it may be their mistake, it creates a negative negotiating environment and slows the overall transaction if the landlord doesn't agree with the terms in the letter of intent and provides a counter.

The letter of intent should contain all the basic financial terms of the transaction as well as any other key terms such as all options, and a notation about the form of lease. This permits the landlord the opportunity to review and comment on all business aspects of the transaction.

We also advise clients to include in the letter of intent and the Offer to Lease the current standard estimate of the operating expenses, realty taxes, premises services costs and any other components that make up the rent. Care must be taken to note that it is only an estimate based at the time of the negotiation.

We have found that including all these numbers is an effective negotiating tool should the tenant want to negotiate the make up and/or allocation of any of these items during the negotiation of the formal lease wording. The landlord can counter the tenant's negotiation by noting that the tenant agreed to the estimate therefore, the tenant must also agree with how that number was derived.

If the tenant presses the issue, the landlord has the opportunity to note the potential shortfall to the original understanding of what the tenant would pay and determine some offsetting compensation, such as an increase in the minimum rent.

Offer to Lease

Unlike the letter of intent, an offer to lease, is legally binding on the parties. It is a formal legal document, typically drafted by knowledgeable lawyers, for all the non-business terms, which can be added in a 'fill in the blanks' type of format; or drafted in its entirety by the lawyer from the information in the letter of intent or deal sheet, if used. An offer to lease contains more information than the letter of intent, but less than a full lease (with a blank lease form attached to the offer).

Whereas, an landlord may wish to go directly from a letter of intent to a lease in an operating property; offers tend to be used more often when the lease itself will commence after a pre-determined date or a series of events, such as when leasing new development to be open in the future.

It is important to the landlord that the lease is negotiated and executed as quickly as possible irrespective of whether the initial document is an offer or letter of intent, and certainly before the landlord invests in the transaction by conducting landlord's work or providing any type of incentive.

Some tenants are masterful at delaying the negotiation and signing of the lease. This can have a serious detrimental impact on the landlord being able to finance the property and on the property value as an offer isn't considered as strong an operating covenant as a lease. Moreover these tenants tend to take a hardline if the landlord presses any point under the terms of the lease by stating that the tenant has not agreed to that lease term (article or clause). They may also note the lease remains open and is in negotiation. To this end, the offer should contain a tight timeline to negotiate and sign a lease, mechanisms to resolve negotiating issues and an outline of what happens if the lease is not executed by a certain time.

Lease Amending Agreements

Anything in the lease or any change in the business relationship that is modified after the original lease is signed must be documented. Failure to do so has left many landlords and tenants in a precarious situation.

While some landlords and tenants have used a simple letter signed by both parties to amend the agreement, we advise that the landlord always use a formal lease amending agreement. Aside from the legal reasons for doing this, the business reasons are important. Informal documents are not well received in the financing and real estate industries. They immediately provoke questions around the professionalism of the landlord and if there are other informal, or undocumented, arrangements.

The only exception to the use of a formal amendment is for very minor housekeeping changes, such as a change in address for either the tenant or the landlord.

Great care should be used in crafting the amending agreement as it forms part of the original lease as though it was in the lease. Likewise, the person drafting the amendment should review the lease to ensure the change doesn't create a conflict elsewhere in the lease.

When negotiating any change to the original lease it is important to remember that the change in the lease arrangement prompts a change in the risk, effectively opening the lease to further negotiation. The party requesting the change is typically in the weaker negotiating position. That noted, if the landlord has the negotiating strength, the landlord should balance any changes they may now want to the lease as a result of the tenant's request to the size and scope of that request. If the landlord overreaches and asks for far more than the tenant perceives as reasonable, the tenant may consider anything in excess as a request from the landlord, giving the tenant negotiating leverage.

This is another reason the landlord wants to review the lease. Certain requests by the tenant, such as an assignment, may trigger conditions the parties agreed to when negotiating the original lease. Don't trust that the person representing the landlord is aware of those conditions on every lease. These are opportunities to obtain full value for those previously negotiated conditions.

Rent Relief

Granting a rent relief is a significant negotiating event and requires a specialized amending agreement. Many times the landlord is presented with a conundrum. The tenant can't pay the full contracted rent for some reason. This leaves the landlord in the position of determining if the lesser of two evils is to modify the rent or obtain vacant possession and find a new tenant. The answer is: "It Depends."

It depends on the general occupancy of the property, co-tenancy agreements, is re-financing coming due, general market conditions, conditions and covenants

224

provided to the lender concerning the current financing, the need for the merchandise mix and many other aspects.

It also depends on whether the rent relief will help the tenant if the situation is already financially fatal to the continuation of the business.

Rent relief is generally provided in two forms:

i. rent abatement, wherein the rent is reduced for a period of time (up to and including the balance of the term of the lease), or

ii. rent deferment. In a deferment, the landlord reduces the rent for a period of time and then recaptures the differential between the contracted rent and the temporary reduction at the end of the rent relief period. The recapture is either a one-time full payment or is completed over time. The landlord must also have confidence in a rent deferment that the tenant will be in a position to repay the rent then due in addition to their regular obligation.

To properly investigate if a rent relief program is prudent, the landlord needs to request specific information from the tenant as well as mine the data the landlord has accumulated.

The information the landlord needs from the tenant is:

- Three years of financial information prepared or certified by a third party.
- A synopsis of the underlying reason for the request.
- A business plan outlining what the tenant is doing to improve the situation.
- A written request concerning the rent relief including how much and for how long it will be needed.
- An indication of what has already been done to fix the issue, and
- Evidence that others, including their lender, are also assisting the tenant.

The evidence of other support is important because the landlord is a supplier just as all the other suppliers and the lender are suppliers of goods and services. The landlord never wants to be the only one receiving less than full value.

The landlord combines this information with the investigation made by them of the market, competitor sales data in the market and in the property (if applicable), a review of other leases for co-tenancy, their own lender provisions concerning occupancy, etc.

The landlord will then be in a position to determine a course of action.

It is rarely advisable that the landlord abate the rent. Here are a few reasons why an abatement should be avoided.

a) The landlord may have provided funding and incentives in consideration of the contracted rent. Abating the rent reduces the effective rent and cashflow.

b) Financial analysts for lenders reviewing the rent schedule for the property may not know this is a special situation and deem the abated rent as market rent for the property. This may affect the landlord's ability to obtain financing.

c) Potential purchasers may deem the property to be in decline due to a reduction in rent, or consider the previous rent as too high and adjust the values down to the level of the abated rent. Again, value is negatively impacted.

d) The new, lower rent may affect other leases that contain a 'market rent' formula in the lease.

e) It may affect the market perception of the property for other lease.

A rent deferent mitigates a number of these concerns, although it won't eliminate them completely. For example, the concern about the effective rent received (item a.) is only eliminated if the deferment is repaid.

The landlord should attach interest to a rent deferment program compounding from the commencement of the deferment to the scheduled end of the repayment period and calculate this into the repayment plan.

No matter if the rent is abated or deferred, the landlord must always bear in mind that the tenant is in financial trouble and could fail. As a result, the landlord should take steps in the rent relief program to minimize their potential risk and losses.

For example, the landlord should retain the ability to seek a replacement tenant for the space that is willing to pay the landlord more rent than the current tenant or has better financial backing.

The landlord should scour the lease for tenant benefit clauses and remove them from the lease as part of the program (see Chapter 9 for more about these types of clauses). The tenant should not be able receive these benefits while paying a reduced rent. These types of clauses can be clawed back for the balance of the lease term, or just for the period of the relief program, as the landlord wishes.

The landlord can expect the tenant to push back on the loss of a restrictive covenant arguing that the landlord shouldn't introduce a competitor while its sales are down. There are a few specific rebuttals to this argument. For one, it is not a foregone conclusion that offering the customer more choice within the category will be detrimental to the tenant's sales. Massing a use in a property can actually draw more customers. Examples include fashion malls, auto malls, outlet centres, electronic centres, food courts, etc.

We also suggest that the landlord retain immediate rights to reinstate the contracted rent as tough no relief program existed if the tenant defaults on any lease provision.

The technique we suggest clients use is neither a rent abatement nor a rent deferment, as they are typically structured.

Instead, we set up the rent relief as a forgivable (in an abatement) or repayable (in a deferment) arrears. Here is how it works.

For the simplicity of the math we will assume that the contracted base rent is $24,000 per annum and the rent relief the landlord is offering is 50% of that - $12,000 for one year.

The base, or minimum rent is not adjusted. It remains at $24,000. However, the landlord agrees with the tenant that it will not collect on that amount for the year. Instead, the amount is allowed to build as an arrear on the tenant's account over the course of the year to $12,000.

There may be some compelling legal reasons under the bankruptcy laws in your area for adopting a similar approach for your property. These should be discussed with a lawyer well versed in the applicable law.

This approach also removes many of the previously cited business concerns.

One final comment on rent relief. The amount and type of relief offered should be restricted to the base or minimum rent only. On the face of it, this seems self explanatory; however, many times landlords have

calculated the relief on the total rent
payable, which includes the cost of operating
the property.

Consents

The initial lease may include various pre-
negotiated requests the tenant may have
over the term of the lease. The two most
common are an assignment and subleasing.

Both these actions require the landlord's
written consent. Both should also contain
conditions that must be met in order for the
landlord to give its consent.

Many landlords and their lawyers create
tripartite agreements comingling the
provisions of the action with the landlord's
consent. For example, the document may
contain the assignment provisions between
the assignor and the assignee; as well as
provisions outlining the landlord's consent to
the assignment.

We don't like this idea because we don't
want anyone to say the landlord knew all the
provisions, intricacies and potential issues
involved in the assignment. The landlord
doesn't want to be party to any errors or
issues between the assignor and assignee.
Instead, the assignment should be between

the two assigning parties and the landlord's consent reserved as a separate document outlining the landlord's consent provisions only. This is the only document to be signed by all.

The same can be said for subleases and any other actions that need the landlord's written consent.

Guaranties, Indemnities and Convenantor Agreements

Although rent guaranties, indemnification agreements and covenantor provisions are usually negotiated at the time of the initial lease negotiation, they are typically attached as stand-alone schedules to the lease and are meant to survive the lease term for the most part.

They can also be introduced into the business relationship during the term of the lease if not originally included, such as when rent relief is granted or an assignment is contemplated.

Although some people use the words rent guaranty, indemnifier and covenantor interchangeably, they are three different legal concepts and have three different meanings depending on the jurisdiction. So please show your lawyer this section and ask for their specific advice. All three have different business implications too.

Without attempting to give a legal definition, the main business differences between the three are:

- A rent guaranty means the payment of the rent itself is guarantied.
- An indemnity agreement means the indemnifier promises performance of the lease by the tenant. Most often this is in the form of financial compensation with no other duty to perform.
- A covenant agreement mandates and allows the covenantor to step into the shoes of the tenant.

The nuances between them may seem subtle but the business aspects are anything but subtle.

In a rent guaranty the rent <u>under the lease</u> is guaranteed to be paid by the person, or entity, providing the guarantee. That entity has no rights to occupy the premises. However, in many instances the guaranty ends if the lease is terminated because there is nothing more to guaranty.

This can place the landlord in a catch 22 position. On one hand the landlord's remedy is termination of the lease after the default period. On the other hand, in some cases the guaranty ends with the termination.

The only way around this is to enact the guaranty before terminating the lease.

An indemnity provision may be a better option. Worded correctly the concept is the indemnifier ensures the performance of the tenant, not the contract per se.

An indemnification can stand the termination of the lease contract. But there may be issues.

The first is that the indemnity is almost always limited to a financial compensation. While this is good for many types of default issues, such as the non-payment of the rent, it doesn't solve all issues.

The second issue is that the indemnification may be invalidated if the landlord doesn't follow all the proper legal protocols. For example, the indemnifier may not have to indemnify the tenant for matters it knew nothing about. As a practical business matter then, the indemnifier should perhaps sign all lease amending and consent agreements. This is something to discuss with your lawyer.

A covenantor may be the best option. In this case, the covenant agreement can be drafted that the covenantor steps into the shoes of the tenant and must perform under the lease as if it was the actual tenant. This solves the first issue of an indemnity. Here are three examples where this may be advantageous to the landlord, over and above the payment of any arrears:

1. Covenantor may remediate any environmental issues left by the tenant,
2. Covenantor may make good any damage caused by the tenant, and
3. Covenantor may operate the tenant's business to avoid co-tenancy issues in other leases or other promises the landlord has granted.

In some cases a covenantor's agreement may be beneficial to the covenantor. For example, we will assume the landlord obtained a covenantor's agreement with the assignor of the lease to another person due to a sale of the business. The vendor also took back a loan as partial payment for the business. However, the purchaser defaults on the lease. The best option for the original tenant, now covenantor, to obtain value may be to step back into the business.

From a business perspective, we believe the very best option for the landlord is the last option combined with indemnification wording.

It is very important to make sure the agreement is properly drafted to reflect both the landlord's intent and the prevailing laws. It is equally important that the landlord consider the agreement non-negotiable otherwise the landlord is both reducing the covenant it receives and increases the risk associated with the transaction.

The landlord (using in-house counsel or their third party legal advisors) should be the ones to draft the document, no matter if the ancillary document is a letter of intent, an offer to lease, an amendment document, a relief program, a consent agreement or a covenantor's agreement. This ensures consistency in the documentation across the property or the portfolio and that the landlord is protected.

IN SUMMARY

All understandings and agreements between the landlord and tenant should be documented.

Any change to the originally negotiated and executed lease should prompt the creation of a lease amending agreement

A rent relief can be structured as an abatement of rent or as a deferment of the rent.

A rent guaranty may create a catch 22 situation for the landlord. A better way of obtaining a form of security is through indemnification and covenantor agreements.

It is prudent for the landlord to maintain drafting control of the agreements irrespective of the document.

Chapter 14
Negotiating Green Leases

Don't let Green turn Red

Green, or sustainability- sensitive, leases promote actions that reduce utility consumption, waste and enhance the operating environment.

From the retail landlord's perspective there is considerable debate in some circles about the need for green leases. Proponents advocate the social responsibility and the reduced operating costs. At the other end of the scale, other landlords believe that the investment produces a poor return due to the structure of the triple net lease.

No matter where you stand on the issue it is important to understand some of the intricacies and pitfalls of green leases because more shopping centres are built with sustainability in mind. In this chapter we will touch on some of the key items to consider in a green lease however, to completely understand the green lease is worthy of in-depth study outside the purpose of this book.

Before discussing green lease negotiations and specific clauses, it is important to note that a multi-tenant property cannot be environmentally responsible by having only some of the leases reflective of 'green' initiatives. The entire property, all tenants and the management must be on board with sustainable operations. This may seem difficult in an existing property but the landlord has three tools they can use, two of which are already imbedded in a typical lease. These tools are:

1. The rules and regulations schedule to the lease.
   The rules and regulations outline some key and property specific operational items, such as when and where to remove waste and trash. They are listed in a schedule as they are meant to be updated and replaced in the lease as required over the term. A good

240

lease provides for this type of updating.

The schedule can be updated to include any new sustainable operating procedures such as detailed recycling initiatives.

2. The Tenant's construction and work schedule to the lease.
   While this schedule cannot be amended in existing leases, it can be amended for future new leasing and renewal options where the tenant is required to refresh and remodel the premises (provided the landlord has used our recommend renewal platform discussed in chapter 7).

   When updating this schedule the landlord can include green building principles they wish in their property.

3. A Memorandum of Understanding (often called a "MoU").
   While not legally binding, the MoU can set out the intent of the parties and include items that would be captured in green lease clauses added to the lease in the future. The purpose of the MoU is to capture a consensus with tenants whose leases do not contain green lease language. The Better

Building Partnership in the United Kingdom has developed a Green Lease Toolkit that incudes a sample of a MoU. (http://www.betterbuildingspartnership.co.uk/working-groups/green-leases/green-lease-toolkit/)

The toolkit also provides direction on how to organize existing tenants and introduce the MoU, which takes a separate negotiation by the property's management, so we won't duplicate their efforts here.

Fundamentals of Negotiating Green Lease Clauses

A green lease does not have a widely accepted definition and can take many forms. What they do have in common are the following key concepts:

(i)   additions to the operating expenses definitions;
(ii) the building of the tenant premises by the tenant (tenant improvements);
(iii) development principles and regulations to promote sustainability;

(iv)   use and disposal of hazardous materials, including cleaning supplies;

(v)   waste and recycling; and

(vi)   an environmental management plan; which will generally include a list of environmentally friendly products to be used by the tenant and those engaged by the tenant for items such as cleaning and HVAC maintenance, water and energy conservation methods and targets, the use of alternative sources of energy on-site as may be implemented by the landlord, indoor air quality standards, and dispute resolution procedures.

The three green leasing standards used in North America are by the Green Building Councils in the USA (http://www.usgbc.org/) and Canada (http://www.cagbc.org), the Building Owners and Managers Association ("BOMA" at http://www.boma.org) and the International Council of Shopping Centres ("ICSC" at http://icsc.org). The green building councils in Canada and the USA as well as the balance of the world administer to the Leadership in Environment and Energy Design ("LEED") programs. These are a strict set of widely accepted standards in the green building industry to certify various levels of sustainable construction and operation. LEED provides all parties with a uniform framework and a third party classification for an environmentally friendly building.

The BOMA and ICSC guides provide landlords and tenants with the framework to enter into a green lease, without the rigidity of the LEED classification and certification process. This is important for two reasons.

    a. The LEED certification process is standardized and expensive as compared to the non-certified options suggested by BOMA and ICSC, and

    b. Failure to maintain a LEED certification can have dramatic consequences.

LEED certification sets targets for both the initial construction or remodeling of a property and the ongoing operation of the property. The more lofty the target the higher the LEED certification.

Certain tenants demonstrate their environmental awareness by leasing in certain minimum LEED classified buildings (such as LEED Silver) and require the landlord to maintain that certification. While this is more an issue in office buildings wishing to attract government tenants, who predominantly have these type of minimum building requirements, similar issues can arise in retail properties.

One of the design and operational targets of LEED buildings is the reduction of energy consumption. An issue arose early in the adoption of LEED when buildings that were certified to a standard due to their design to operate at a certain energy consumption level failed to meet those levels after opening. The failure was caused by a change in the use and occupancy of the building as compared to when it was originally designed. The building no longer met the minimum LEED certification. To combat the potential of buildings being designed to and receiving LEED certification, but then not maintaining its operational design the LEED program was modified to mandate the landlords to periodically report on its energy efficiency.

This is problematic in the context of a multi-tenant shopping centre for a number of reasons.

It requires that the tenants, who may have individual utility metering, to provide consumption information to the landlord. This adds administrative time for both the tenant and the landlord.

The changing nature of the tenancy in each space means the energy consumption is not predictable. One tenant may use little water or electricity whereas another may use a lot more as compared to either the previous tenant or the average of the property solely based on the nature of their use.

Tenants with multiple locations want consistency in their design and public persona, which may not be compatible with a rigid standard at a particular property.

Due to these reasons, many developers and landlords of retail properties use a standard other than the LEED certification process. Irrespective of which standard the landlord uses, the lease should never specify a standard or level for these reasons. Instead the lease should speak in general terms about the importance of sustainability and actions toward that goal.

Obviously, if the lease does speak to a certain level, such as LEED Silver, then the lease needs language that addresses the issues above as well as consequences for not meeting the operational criteria to maintain the standard.

Here are some typical green oriented clause concepts that should be included in the lease.

The definitions section of the lease needs to be expanded to capture accepted green terminology.

A co-operation agreement clause sets the frame against which the other clauses can be interpreted.

The landlord may want to convene a Green or Building Management Group made up of tenants and the management to discuss ongoing sustainable ideas and programs. The clause would be much the same as the concept of a merchants association forming marketing and promotional plans. These types of groups are not mandatory, but if used, the lease should include a provision both for the existence and participation in the group.

If the tenant spaces have direct utility metering, then there needs to be a clause about data-sharing. Typically this is a mutual sharing arrangement, whereby the tenant shares specific information about their consumption and the landlord shares property wide information.

An expansion of the Landlord's rights to work and inspect the premises. This clause is required when the tenant refuses to cooperate in providing metering, etc. Because a green building requires all parties to be in the program, and not just some, the landlord needs the option to unilaterally act if it is in the best interests of the landlord's business objectives and the direction of the property.

To reiterate what was noted before, the tenant must comply with the standards set if there is a certification in place and must not make alterations to the approved design of the premises. This should be included in the lease and the tenant work schedule.

The provisions allowing the removal of tenant installations needs to be expanded so that any installation made to the premises relative to enhancing sustainability and reducing energy consumption must remain. There are a host of reasons for this, and it is also a practical point in the ongoing operation of the property. Note that this does not include chattels.

Finally, the dispute resolution clause may need to be expanded specifically for the green clauses and the use of experts in sustainable building design and operation to mediate as compared to a typical arbitrator.

IN SUMMARY

There is no one definition of a "Green" lease and there are various different standards and criteria that can be used.

Green leases built upon a standard lease document by adding clauses, and sometimes, additional wording to existing clauses.

Having an environmentally friendly property means all tenants must be on the same page and that understanding needs to be committed to a document.

Significant issues can arise if the landlord commits to a certain standard in the lease and that standard is not maintained, even if the root cause of not maintaining the standard is in a tenant's operation of its business.

Chapter 15
Considerations in Mixed Use Projects

Early decisions will affect the leasing process and profitability of a Mixed-Use project

Any property that houses more than one asset class is a mixed use project, even if it is as simple as a second floor office space above a retail strip centre. Mixed use projects have been in existence for many years, even if they were called a mixed use development. More recently however, the concept of a property containing a variety of commercial asset classes has moved to the forefront. This is due, in part, to the number of uses being placed together in a very dense site. One doesn't have to look very far to find examples of a large retail development that also has a residential segment that is either rental or set up as a condominium (or both), hospitality, office and entertainment.

The more the different asset classes in one property the more difficult the administration becomes, more complicated the lease becomes and the lease negotiations also become more complicated.

Notwithstanding the complexity, society seems to be embracing the convenience of living, working and playing in a compact area. And even in it's simplest forms the concept can be more beneficial to the landlord than a single use property. Anecdotal comments from developers seem to suggest that there is a premium pricing potential for each use based upon the other uses being in the property; although no formal study could be found to support these claims. Developers we spoke to, for example, indicated that the presence of a substantial residential component allowed the developer to charge more for the retail minimum rent, and a well merchandised retail component in the same project allowed the landlord to charge more for the residential portion.

Due to the complexity of administering to the different uses in the property, the different lease and ownership structures that can occur and the appropriate apportionment of the costs (from development through to operating) and, in some cases, differing regulations affecting the legal aspects of each component, the subject of attending to all of these relative to a retail lease negotiation deserves it's own book.

That said, there are some key concepts worth noting here for the smaller, easier to manage properties such as the strip centre we describe in the introduction to this chapter.

The overarching concept is that each asset class has its own dynamics. Therefore, the property should not be considered a homogenous unit. Instead, it should be perceived by the landlord, leased, operated and administered as the aggregate of separate units on one hand; and as a divisible unit on the other. What do we mean by this?

While some aspects of the property are common to all the asset classes, such a perimeter landscaping, utility mains, etc. other aspects pertain to a specific use and should be separate from each other. Still other aspects can become very complicated, such as apportioned and common parking, which crosses over between the two.

The landlord needs to carefully consider the interplay between each asset type from the start of development through the entire life cycle of the property. This needs to be reflected in the different lease types used for the property. It is prudent to use different leases for each commercial asset type (ie: retail, office, apartment) and reciprocal operating agreements across the property.

The lease in each case needs to both define the scope of the asset class and how the various asset classes and the common areas interact. Following is a simple example.

The property has a building surrounded by common parking and landscape. The ground floor is retail space. The second floor, accessed by stairs and an elevator, is office space. The second floor office space covers 50% of the main floor area.

The landlord may wish to define the shopping centre *building* as the main floor in the retail lease, exclusive of the elevator and stair vestibule. Conversely, the landlord may wish to define the office *building* separately inclusive of the elevator and stairs. Then the landlord may wish to have the parking lot and landscaping as common to both. Furthermore the landlord may allocate costs relative to the roof over the office area as pertaining to that area alone or combine the two roofs and have them divisible by both the office and retail areas.

In this example, the leases for each of the retail and office areas needs to reflect definitions for each of:

- the shopping centre;
- the office portion of the building and
- the property.

As well, the operating costs need to be separated in the lease and various cost "pools" defined. There also needs to be cross easements.

Of course this is a very simplified version of all the considerations that need to go into the appropriate leases.

The leases for each use type also need to be carefully reviewed to ensure there are no inadvertent conflicts between them.

When structuring the various leases and operating agreements, it is sometimes easier to start with the big picture - in our example, that was the parking lot and the landscape areas - and step into each asset class, rather than start with an asset class and build the agreements up from there.

The landlord may find the exercise easier if the development is situated horizontally across the land, with each type of use occupying it's own part of the overall property; rather than the various uses occupying different air parcels in a vertical development with an abundance of shared services.

It is always wise to use a third party consulting firm with extensive experience in mixed use projects, such as us, to review the project from the outset. Ideally, the firm should be engaged at the same time as the architect so the two can work together in developing the construction and determining how the entire development will work together. There is considerable thought, planning and work to be done at the very start of the project, beyond the drawings and construction, which will save time and money and mitigate risk later in the project.

The landlord can expect tenants to extensively question the method of allocation between the asset types and to attempt to negotiate both the allocations to the shopping centre vs. other components of the property and the costs within the shopping centre.

Tenants will also attempt to seek opening and co-tenancy agreements within both the shopping centre and the larger development. If it is expected that this will be a new, phased development, tenants will want to understand and commit the developer to the timeframe for construction, the construction details (such as access, noise, signage, etc.) and consequences for missing deadlines, business interruption, etc.

There are no hard and fast negotiating rules or techniques regarding these issues that aren't already reviewed in this book. The specific issues, challenges and negotiating points will vary because the nature of each mixed-use development is different.

There are also different legal requirements depending on where the project is located, and if the development is owned entirely by one entity or if different parts of the overall project are owned by different entities, such as in a strata (also known as a 'condo') development.

Another reason to engage an experienced mixed-use consultant early in the development phase is directly related to the leasing of the retail portion.

By its very nature, retail is a very dynamic asset class and as such the retail portion can have an effect on the balance of the project. To illustrate the point consider just these two issues: traffic flow of vehicles and people around and through the project and the merchandising mix of the retail area.

Special consideration needs to be given to such details as vertical transportation in a stacked mix-use project, such as those in dense urban areas. The landlord doesn't want residents, for example, sharing the same elevator used to access the grocery store on the property due to congestion and different hours of use, or having residents rely on a general freight elevator to move their furniture in and out that is also used by restaurants to transport messy grease waste.

The landlord is inviting ongoing complaints and managerial issues when merchandising the retail portion and specifying restaurant space in the leasing plan whose kitchen exhaust will be next to the main ventilation intake duct for the residential portion of the project. It happens.

Since retail is probably the most dynamic of the asset classes represented in most mixed use projects there is a further consideration that the developer and any landlord buying the retail portion of the project needs to be aware of if the property involves a strata.

It is important that how the strata is structured that the retail portion controls the overall project; otherwise, it is possible that one of the other uses (such as residents in a condominium) could dictate how the retail portion is leased and operates. This could be disastrous to the viability of the retail component and the leasing efforts.

IN SUMMARY

Mixed-use developments require specialized expertise to develop the leases and operational program. This should be engaged near the very beginning of the process to save time and money and avoid mistakes.

Each use type should have its own lease form but all documents should reference and retain consistency between them to avoid wording conflicts.

The landlord needs to lease and operate the project as a collection of different uses, each with its own requirements; rather than one homogenous, and identical project.

INDEX

U

V

ABOUT

Peter D. Morris CRX, SCLS, SCSM, SCMD is a certified and recognized retail property expert holding multiple senior accreditations in the leasing, management and marketing of retail properties. In fact, at the time of publication of this book he is one of only 25 people worldwide with all these designations.

In a career that has spanned more than three decades, Mr. Morris has worked globally in 8 countries and lived in three to bring a unique global perspective. He has worked for institutional owners such as Cadillac Fairview and Brookfield Properties and was the Chief Operating Officer of Partners Real Estate Investment Trust; as well as in a third party capacity as Senior Vice President with Colliers International. As one client aptly said: "I know what I know, but Peter knows what the global industry knows."

Previously, he was a retailer so he provides a 360^0 view of a negotiation.

He has presented across North America, Asia, the Middle East and South America. In addition he was on the editorial board of a New York shopping centre specialty publication and has been a frequent industry contributor, college lecturer, expert witness and industry commentator and panelist.

Want More Information?

Maximize the value of the **Masterguide to Leasing for Retail Landlords** ™ by booking Mr. Morris to speak to your organization.

For more information please contact Peter Morris directly at pdmorris@greensteadcg.com

Coming Soon
Other Publications by Peter D. Morris

Masterguide to Leasing for Office Landlords™

Masterguide to Leasing for Retail Tenants™

Masterguide to Leasing for Office Tenants™